# CHURCH OF THE NAZARENE

## CHILDREN'S BIBLE QUIZZING MINISTRY

# Genesis

"IN THE BEGINNING GOD CREATED
THE HEAVENS AND THE EARTH."
GENESIS 1:1

## CHILDREN'S BIBLE STUDY AND BIBLE QUIZZING
## FROM 7 - 11 YEARS
## NIV BIBLE

CBQM

C

CHILDREN'S BIBLE
QUIZZING MINISTRY

Children's Bible Quizzing Ministry - Genesis

Published by: Discipleship Ministries of the Mesoamerica Region

www.discipleship.MesoamericaRegion.org

www.SdmiResources.MesoamericaRegion.org

ISBN: 978-1-63580-166-8

The people who participated in the original idea and production of the games and activities portion of this book are:
Carolina Ambrosio
Eva Velazquez
Patricia Picavea
Patricia Zamora

Adapted by: Pamela Vargas Castillo, with love for the children of the Church of the Nazarene

Printed in the United States

# Welcome to the marvelous ministry of Children's Bible Quizzing

## In this book you will find:

1.  Bible Study Lessons and basic questions (p. 4)

2.  Guide for leading Children's Bible Quizzing using games and activities (p. 49)

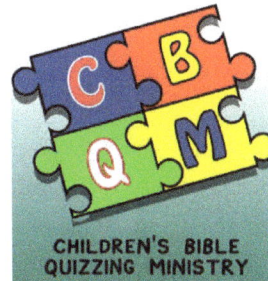

3.  Guide for leading Children's Bible Quizzing using questions and answers (p. 110)

**NOTE:** It's important that you work with only one type of quizzing for competitions.

# CONTENTS

# WELCOME!

Welcome to Bible Studies for Children: Genesis! In this collection of biblical studies, the children will learn about God's holiness and his faithfulness to his people, even when they make a bad choice.

Bible Studies for Children: Genesis is one of six books in the Bible Studies for Children series. These studies help children to gain an understanding of biblical chronology and the meaning of biblical events. As the children learn about the lives of the people in these studies, they discover God's love for all people and their place in his plan. God sometimes uses miracles to achieve his purposes. He often works through people to accomplish what he wants to do.

The philosophy of Bible Studies for Children is to help the children to understand what the Bible says, to learn how God helped the people, and to know God through a relationship with him. This includes biblical study, biblical memorization, and application of biblical teachings in real life situations.

Bible Studies for Children uses the New International Version of the Bible.

## BOOKS

The following is a short description of the books in this series and the way that they interact with each other.

**Genesis** provides the foundation. This book tells how God created the world from nothing, formed a man and a woman, and created a beautiful garden for their home. These people sinned, and they experienced the consequences for their sin. Genesis introduces the plan of God to reconcile the broken relationship between God and the people. It introduces Adam, Eve, Noah, Abraham, Isaac, and Jacob.

God made a covenant with Abraham and renewed that covenant with Isaac and Jacob. Genesis ends with the story of Joseph who saves civilization from famine. The famine compels the people of God to move to Egypt.

**Exodus** tells how God continued to keep his promise to Abraham. God rescued the Israelites from slavery in Egypt. The Lord chose Moses to guide the Israelites. The Lord set up his kingship over the Israelites. He led and ruled the Israelites through the establishment of the priesthood and the Tabernacle, the Ten Commandments and other laws, and the prophets and the judges. At the end of Exodus, only a part of the covenant of the Lord with Abraham is complete.

**Joshua/Judges/Ruth** tells how God completed his covenant with Abraham that began in Genesis. The Israelites conquered and settled into the land that God promised to Abraham.

The prophets, the priests, the Law, and the worship rituals declared that God was the Lord and the King of the Israelites. The 12 tribes of Israel settled into the Promised Land. This study emphasizes these judges: Deborah, Gideon, and Samson.

In **1 and 2 Samuel**, the Israelites wanted a king because the other nations had a king. These books tell about Samuel, Saul, and David. Jerusalem became the center of the combined nation of Israel. This study shows how the people reacted differently when someone confronted them with their sins. While Saul blamed others or made excuses, David admitted his sin, and he asked God for forgiveness.

**Matthew** is the focal point of the entire series. It focuses on the birth, the life, and the ministry of Jesus. All the previous books in the series pointed to Jesus as the Son of God and the Messiah. Jesus ushered in a new era. The children learn about this new era in several events: the teachings of Jesus, his death, his resurrection, and the mentoring of his disciples. Through Jesus, God provided a new way for the people to have a relationship with him.

At the beginning of **Acts**, Jesus ascended to heaven, and God sent the Holy Spirit to help the Church. The good news of salvation through Jesus Christ spread to many parts of the world. The believers preached the gospel to the Gentiles, and missionary work began. The message of the love of God transformed both the Jews and the Gentiles. There is a direct connection between the evangelism efforts of Paul and Peter to the lives of the people today.

## CYCLE

The following cycle of this series is specifically for those who participate in the optional Bible Quizzing aspect of Bible Studies for Children.

You will find more information about this in the section called "Children's Bible Quizzing" (page 48).

- Genesis (2019-2020)
- Exodus (2020-2021)
- Joshua, Judges and Ruth (2021-2022)
- 1 & 2 Samuel (2022-2023)
- Matthew (2023-2024)
- Acts (2024-2025)

## SCHEDULE

Each book of the series has about 20 lessons. Each lesson is designed for 1 to 2 hours for class time. The following Schedule is one suggestion for each study:

- 15 minutes for the Activity
- 30 minutes for the Bible Lesson
- 15 minutes for the Memory Verse
- 30 minutes for Additional Activities (optional)
- 30 minutes for practicing the Bible Quizzing (optional)

# PREPARATION FOR THE TEACHER

Thorough preparation of each study is important. The children are more attentive and gain better understanding of the study if you prepare it well and present it well. The following steps will help you prepare.

**Step 1: Bible Passage and Bible Commentary.** Read the verses of the Biblical Passage for the lesson and the information of the Biblical Commentary, as well as the Words related to our Faith, People, Places, and Objects that are included.

**Step 2: Opening Activity.** This section includes a game or other activity with the goal of preparing the children for the Bible lesson. Familiarize yourself with the activity, the instructions, and the materials. Take the materials that you'll need to class. Prepare the activity before the children arrive.

**Step 3: Bible Lesson.** Review the lesson and learn it so that you tell it as a story. The children want the teacher to tell the story rather than to read it from the book.

Use the Words of Our Faith from each lesson to provide additional information as you tell the story. After the story, use the review questions. They will help the children to understand the story and to apply it to their lives.

**Paso 4: Memory Verse (Key Verse).** Learn the memory verse (p. 111) before you teach the children. On page 110, there are suggestions for memorization. Choose from the activities to help the children learn the memory verse. Become familiar with the activity that you choose. Read the instructions and prepare the supplies that you will bring to class.

**Step 5: Suggested Activities.**

The Suggested Activities reinforce the Children's Bible Study using games and activities (included in this book). Many of these activities require additional supplies, resources, and time.

Become familiar with the activities that you choose. Read the instructions and prepare the supplies that you will bring to class.

**Step 6: Review the questions about the study**

**Step 7 (Optional): Practice for the Bible Quizzing Competition using the method of questions and answers.** This is a type of competition of Bible Studies for children. More information can be found in the section titled, "Guide for Bible Quizzing using Questions and Answers" (p. 113). If you decide to participate in this type of quizzing, spend time with the children in preparation. There are practice questions for each study. The first 10 questions are for the basic level of competition, and are found after each Bible Study. The 10 questions for the advanced level of competition can be found at the end of the book (p. 120). With the guidance of the teacher, the children choose their level of competition.

# LESSON 1

## Genesis 1:1-31; 2:2-3, 7
## In the Beginning

**MEMORY VERSE:** "In the beginning God created the heavens and the earth." (Genesis 1:1).

**BIBLICAL TRUTH:** God is the creator of the world.

### BIBLICAL COMMENTARY

Creation displays the power of God. God spoke the words, and the lifeless planet responded. God's creation brought life out of emptiness and order from chaos. God called to creation and creation responded. This is God's first commandment.

God invited creation to come into being for delight and enjoyment, and "it was so". Similarly, creation eagerly responded with gratitude and delight.

Genesis 1:26-27 refers to the involvement of God the Father, the Son, and the Holy Spirit in creation.

God did not create everything haphazardly. Instead, everything has a purpose. People are most happy when they serve a noble purpose or work for something greater than themselves. In Genesis 2 and 3, we learn that God trusted the man and woman to take care of his special garden. This was an important task. It was not drudgery for Adam and Eve. They were content with their job.

From the beginning, God acted for the good of creation. To the man he gave a beautiful home and good food. He gave a caretaker to the garden. He warned Adam of the danger. He gave a helper to Adam.

God also set an example for people by resting on the seventh day. This does not imply that God was tired. Creation was complete, and God was content with what he created. He is also satisfied when the creation turns its attention to the creator. When Christians observe the Sabbath, it indicates their faith and trust in God. Resting reminds us, the created, to submit our will to God, the creator.

### WORDS OF OUR FAITH

**man** -- humanity. God made a male and a female. Together he called them man or mankind. They were both created in the image of God.

### ACTIVITY

Before the children arrive, choose an outside location for this activity. You will lead the children on a nature walk to this location. Find a space for the children to sit so that they will be able to discuss what they see.

During the class, say, **Today we will take a nature walk. As we walk, look at everything around you. Think about what you see: the sky, the grass, the flowers, the birds, the animals, and the people.**

Lead the children to the location you chose. Encourage the children to share with the class the things they saw as they walked.

Say, **The Bible is a book that tells the story of God. The book of Genesis tells us that God created the world. God created the ground where we sit. He created the sky above our heads. God created the plants, the trees, and the flowers. God created the animals. He also created people.**

Pray with the children. Thank God for everything he created. In your prayer, say the name of each child and thank God for him or her. Then return to the classroom.

### BIBLICAL LESSON

Prepare a Bible story based on the lesson's scripture verses. Children will understand the lesson better if you tell them the story rather than reading it to them.

After the story, encourage the children to discuss the story by asking the following questions. This will help them apply it to their lives. There may not be a right or wrong answer.

1. What would you say to God if you watched him create everything on the earth?

2. How did God create people differently from the rest of creation? How does that difference make you feel about God?

3. God set the example for us on the seventh day. He rested. Do you like to rest? Do you think it is important? Why or why not?

4. What is the most important idea in the memory verse, Genesis 1:1?

Say, **Close your eyes and think about your favorite animal, your favorite color, your favorite fruit, your best friend, and a family member. God created col ours, plants, animals, and people.**

**God is powerful and creative. The Bible says that God cares for everything he made. God made people. God created people to have a relationship with him. You can praise God because he is the Creator of the entire universe, and he cares for you.**

## MEMORY VERSE

Practice the study's memory verse. You will find suggestions for memory verse activities on page 110.

## ADDITIONAL ACTIVITIES

Choose from these options to enhance the children's Bible study.

1. Create an art project about creation, including papier-mâché models, clay figures, dioramas, paintings, posters, murals, or chalk drawings. Provide the children with a variety of craft supplies. Encourage the children to be creative.

2. Ask the children about how God created the world. Then, discuss with them why it is more important that we understand the one who created everything is more important than how it was done.

3. Do a game or activity in the following section that relates to this lesson (p. 49ff).

## BASIC QUESTIONS

1. *Who created the heavens and the earth? (1:1)*
    1. Man
    **2. God**
    3. No one

2. *What did God create on the first day? (1:3, 5)*
    1. Sea life
    2. Plants and trees
    **3. Light**

3. *What did God do on the second day? (1:7-8)*
    1. Created the stars
    **2. Separated the waters**
    3. Created man

4. *What did God tell the land to produce on the third day? (1:11, 13)*
    1. Livestock and wild animals
    **2. Trees and plants**
    3. Both answers are correct.

5. *Why did God create the greater lights and the lesser lights? (1:14-18)*
    1. To separate the day from the night
    2. To mark the seasons
    **3. Both answers are correct.**

6. *When did God create birds? (1:20, 23)*
    1. The third day
    2. The fourth day
    **3. The fifth day**

7. *How did God create man? (1:26-27)*
    1. From the water of the ocean
    2. From the clouds of the sky
    **3. In the image of God**

8. *What did God give to the man and the woman to eat? (1:29)*
    1. Meat
    **2. Seed-bearing plants and fruit**
    3. Both answers are correct.

9. *What did God do on the seventh day? (2:2-3)*
    1. God blessed the day and called it holy.
    2. God rested.
    **3. Both answers are correct.**

10. *From what did God form man? (2:7)*
    **1. From the dust of the ground**
    2. From the air
    3. Both answers are correct.

# LESSON 2

## Genesis 2:15-25; 3:1-24
## The Problem of Sin

**MEMORY VERSE:** "So God created mankind in his own image, in the image of God he created them; male and female he created them." (Genesis 1:27)

**BIBLICAL TRUTH:** God wants to have a close relationship with us.

## BIBLICAL COMMENTARY

Adam and Eve were part of God's creation and lived in a close relationship with God. Adam and Eve used their God-given ability to make choices. However, Adam and Eve made a poor choice, and they suffered the consequences of their choice. They were no longer allowed to live in the goodness of the garden.

When we choose our own way rather than the way of God, we experience guilt, and our selfishness is exposed. Often, we attempt to hide from God, but this does not make our pitiful situation better. Only God can bring reconciliation. He makes this possible through his prevenient grace.

Prevenient grace is when God acts on our behalf or reaches out to us before we even think about him or ask him for anything. Grace means "gift of God." Prevenient grace makes it possible for us to want to seek God.

People have the freedom to choose between right and wrong. Because sin is such a big part of our world, we most often choose wrongly. This is not the type of world God intended. He is working through people to set things right. God's prevenient grace encourages us to draw near to him instead.

## WORDS OF OUR FAITH

- **to sin** -- to disobey God. We sin when we put our will above God's will. Sin can refer to a person's nature or to an action. We sin when we do something that God said not to do. We also sin when we fail to do what God said to do.

## ACTIVITY

You will need these items for this activity:
- some small pieces of paper
- a large piece of paper and a marker. If you have access to a board, then you need to have chalk or a marker.
- question cards (see below for instructions)
- tape to affix the cards to the board

Before class, draw a large fruit tree on the board.

To prepare question cards, write the number "100" on a card or piece of paper. Write the number "200" on another card, then write the number "300" on another card. Continue this pattern (100, 200, 300) for each question. On the other side of each card, write one of the questions that follow. You may want to write a few more questions of your own to give children more opportunities. Attach these cards to the tree with only the number side of the card showing.

Say, **Today you will learn about Adam, Eve, the serpent, and the choices that Adam and Eve made. Each team may pick a "fruit" from the tree. If you answer the question on the paper correctly, your team will receive the points indicated on that paper.**

Divide the group into two teams and begin the game. Encourage the children to help their teammates answer the questions. Keep score of the points.

Questions:
1. **Who created the world?** (God)
2. **What did God call the dry ground?** (land)
3. **What did God call the gathered waters?** (seas)
4. **What did God breathe into the first man?** (breath of life)
5. **When did God create the animals?** (sixth day)
6. **From what did God make the man?** (the dust of the ground)
7. **What did God create on the seventh day?** (nothing, he rested; he created the Sabbath, a day for rest)
8. **In whose image did God create the people?** (in his image)

## BIBLICAL LESSON

Prepare a Bible story based on the lesson's scripture verses. Children will understand the lesson better if you tell them the story rather than reading it to them.

After the story, encourage the children to discuss the story by asking the following questions. This will help them apply it to their lives. There may not be a right or wrong answer.

1. **What did Adam and Eve do when they heard God in the garden? Have you ever tried to hide from someone after you disobeyed? How did you feel?**

2. **Who or what is cursed because of the actions of Adam and Eve? Do you think sin affects only the person who committed the sin? Explain your answer.**

3. **Why did God banish the couple from the garden?**

4. **How does today's memory verse, Genesis 1:27, relate to this story and to our lives?**

Say, **God created all things for good purposes. But Adam and Eve chose not to trust God. They thought they knew what was best. So, they disobeyed God. Adam and Eve made a bad decision, and that is bad news. The good news is that God wanted to repair his relationship with Adam and Eve. God does that with us too. Even when we disobey God, God wants to repair the relationship. If God can work with Adam and Eve, God can work with you.**

## MEMORY VERSE

Practice the study's memory verse. You will find suggestions for memory verse activities on pages 110.

## ADDITIONAL ACTIVITIES

Choose from these options to enhance the children's Bible study.

1. Ask, **What are some freedoms your parents allow you now? How can your choices influence your freedoms?** With the class, create a chart with three columns. In the middle, record a list of freedoms the children have. On the left, write down choices which may negatively affect their freedom. On the right, record choices which may positively affect their freedom. Say, **Let's ask God to help us to make choices that he thinks are best.**

2. Use modern maps to find the Tigris and Euphrates Rivers. Ask, **Can you guess where the Garden of Eden may have been?** (Some scholars suggest southern Iraq, but no one knows for sure.)

3. Do a game or activity in the following section that relates to this lesson (p. 49ff).

## BASIC QUESTIONS

1. *What was Adam's job in the Garden of Eden? (2:15-20)*
   1. He worked and cared for the garden
   2. He named all the animals.
   3. **Both answers are correct.**

2. *Why did God create a woman for the man? (2:18, 20)*
   1. **It was not good for the man to be alone.**
   2. Adam did not like any of the animals.
   3. Both answers are correct.

3. *What did the serpent say to Eve about God's commands? (3:1)*
   1. "It is OK to eat from any tree."
   2. "God wanted me to tell you not to eat any fruit."
   3. **"Did God really say, 'You must not eat from any tree in the garden'?"**

4. *Who was the first to eat the fruit? (3:6)*
   1. The serpent
   2. The man
   3. **The woman**

5. *Why did Adam and Eve hide from God? (3:8-10)*
   1. They were afraid because they stole the fruit.
   2. **They were afraid because they were naked.**
   3. Both answers are correct.

6. *Whom did the man blame when God asked if he ate from the tree? (3:11-12)*
   1. **The woman (Eve)**
   2. Himself
   3. The serpent

7. *What happened to the serpent (3:14)*
   1. God blessed the serpent.
   2. **God cursed the serpent.**
   3. The woman cared for the serpent.

8. *How did Adam obtain the garments of animal skins? (3:21)*
   1. **God made them.**
   2. Adam made them.
   3. Eve made them.

9. *What happened after God made garments for Adam & Eve?*
   1. God said, "The man has now become like one of us."
   2. God banished them from the Garden of Eden.
   3. **Both answers are correct.**

10. *With what did God guard the way to the tree of life? (3:24)*
    1. The serpent
    2. **The cherubim and a flaming sword**
    3. Both answers are correct

# LESSON 3

## Genesis 4:1-16; 25-26
## Cain's Conflict

**MEMORY VERSE:** "But if you do not do what is right, sin is crouching at your door; it desires to have you, but you must rule over it." (Genesis 4:7b)

**BIBLICAL TRUTH:** God is both holy and merciful.

### BIBLICAL COMMENTARY

Cain and Abel lived outside of the Garden of Eden. Abel became a shepherd and tended flocks, while Cain became a farmer. The Bible does not say why Cain's offering displeased God. However, the Bible does make it clear that Cain had the opportunity to make a right choice. Cain was free and capable of faithfulness.

Verses five and six define Cain's source of trouble. He was angry. But Cain was not angry at his brother for bringing the sacrifice of the firstborn flock. No, he was angry at God for not accepting his offering of fruits of the soil. God acted in a way that Cain did not understand. However God reminded Cain that he had a choice. He could change his attitude toward God and his brother and do well. Or he could succumb to his anger.

In verse seven, the Bible uses vivid imagery to describe sin. This verse compares sin to a predator stalking its prey. Sin is portrayed in this passage as conniving and vicious. God warned Cain that his thoughts and anger were dangerous. Unfortunately, Cain did not listen to God. He chose instead to give in to his thoughts of destruction.

At the end of the story, Cain is marked by God. This mark indicates Cain's guilt. However, it is also a sign of God's mercy. God spared his life by keeping anyone from killing him.

### WORDS OF OUR FAITH

- **to show mercy** -- to extend forgiveness or kindness to someone who has done wrong.

### ACTIVITY

You will need the following items for this activity:

- stackable blocks (wooden or cardboard)
- small pieces of paper
- a pen or a pencil
- clear tape

Before class, write the following words on small pieces of paper: selfishness, anger, and jealousy. Make several sets. Make a tower with the stackable blocks. Tape the pieces of paper with words on them to several of the blocks.

Say, **Today we will learn how wrong attitudes can affect relationships. Each person will receive an opportunity to remove a block. How many blocks can we remove and keep the tower standing?**

Play a few rounds. Say, **Some blocks had words on them. What were they?** Allow children to respond. **Today we will learn about Cain. Cain struggled with wrong attitudes, such as anger, selfishness, and jealousy. These attitudes ruin relationships. When you removed blocks from the tower, it fell. When a person has wrong attitudes, they ruin the relationship with God.**

### BIBLICAL LESSON

Prepare a Bible story based on the lesson's scripture verses. Children will understand the lesson better if you tell them the story rather than reading it to them.

After the story, encourage the children to discuss the story by asking the following questions. This will help them apply it to their lives. There may not be a right or wrong answer.

1. **Why was Cain angry?**

2. **God helped Cain to see that he had a choice regarding his attitude. If Cain changed his attitude, how would the story be different?**

3. Have you ever struggled with jealousy or anger in your family? How did you deal with it?

4. How does today's memory verse, Genesis 4:7b, relate to this story and to your life?

Cain had a bad attitude. He did not ask God to forgive him. Instead, Cain vented his anger on his brother. God punished Cain because he killed Abel. The Bible says not to sin "in your anger" (see Ephesians 4:26). That means, if you are angry, do not act out your anger and hurt someone or yourself. Cain had the opportunity to ask God for help, but he did not. God knows that we struggle with anger and jealousy, and God wants to help us overcome these problems.

## MEMORY VERSE

Practice the study's memory verse. You will find suggestions for memory verse activities on pages 110.

## ADDITIONAL ACTIVITIES

Choose from these options to enhance the children's Bible study.

1. Research various Old Testament worship and sacrifice rituals. Read Leviticus 1—7 to learn about these sacrificial offerings and their meanings: burnt offering, grain offering, fellowship offering, and sin offering.

2. Discuss this question: Who suffers most from feelings of anger and hate? Is it you or the person whom you hate? When you are angry, what happens to your stomach and intestines? Is this good for your body? What could happen to your body after a long period of time? What could you do instead of hating?

3. Play a game or do an activity from the following section that relates to this lesson (p. 49ff).

# BASIC QUESTIONS

1. *Who was the oldest son of Adam and Eve? (4:1-2)*
   1. Abel
   2. Seth
   3. **Cain**

2. *What was Cain's job? (4:2)*
   1. Shepherd
   2. **Farmer**
   3. Fisherman

3. *What was Abel's job? (4:2)*
   1. Fisherman
   2. Farmer
   3. **Shepherd**

4. *Who pleased the Lord with his offering? (4:4)*
   1. Cain
   2. Adam
   3. **Abel**

5. *What made Cain angry? (4:4-5)*
   1. The Lord did not look with favor on his offering.
   2. The Lord looked with favor on Abel's offering.
   3. **Both answers are correct.**

6. *What did the Lord say that Cain must master? (4:7)*
   1. Gardening
   2. **Sin**
   3. Both answers are correct.

7. *Why did the Lord punish Cain? (4:8-11)*
   1. **Cain attacked and killed Abel.**
   2. Cain offered fish to the Lord.
   3. Cain did not want to be a farmer.

8. *What was Cain's punishment? (4:11-12)*
   1. **The ground would not grow crops for him.**
   2. He could never leave the Garden of Eden.
   3. Both answers are correct.

9. *Where did Cain go when he left the garden? (4:16)*
   1. The land of Nod
   2. East of Eden
   3. **Both answers are correct.**

10. *When did people begin to call on the name of the Lord? (4:26)*
    1. When they heard that Abel was dead
    2. Before Abel was born
    3. **About the time that Seth's son was born**

# LESSON 4

## Genesis 6:5-7:16
## One Man Obeys

**MEMORY VERSE:** "Noah was a righteous man, blameless among the people of his time, and he walked faithfully with God." (Genesis 6:9b)

**BIBLICAL TRUTH:** God is with you, even if you think that you are the only person who obeys him.

## BIBLICAL COMMENTARY

The story of Noah and the flood is one of the most well-known stories of the Bible. Genesis 6 describes a time when the people were very evil and wicked. When God looked into the heart of mankind, he saw "only evil all the time." Verse six says that the heart of the Lord was "deeply troubled." The wickedness of mankind pained God's heart. God would not tolerate this wretched creation as it was. He would blot out the corruption and the violence. God's creation had no regard for him and were going their own way. God judged and condemned the earth.

However, at this point in the story where God lost hope for the world, Genesis 6:8 includes a critical transitional statement: "But Noah found favor in the eyes of the Lord." Because of Noah, another plan was possible. God invited Noah to be a part of it. God told Noah the plan and gave Noah specific instructions. This time God attempted a new covenant with the only one who continued to walk with him. Thanks to Noah's righteousness, he and his family were spared.

So while all of creation was perverse, God found someone who still followed him. In verses 6:22 and 7:5 we discover the character of Noah as he listened and obeyed. God changed his position toward humanity.

## WORDS OF OUR FAITH

*   **righteous** -- to be in right relationship with God and to obey him because of that relationship. To be righteous is to be like Christ in thoughts, words, and actions.

## ACTIVITY

You will need these items for this activity:

*   a tape measure
*   four pylons or some other objects to mark the corners of the ark
*   a very large area
*   small pieces of paper
*   a pen or a pencil

Before class, if possible, find an area to measure and mark the size of Noah's ark. Use pylons or other objects to mark the corners of the area. The ark was approximately 140 meters long, 23 meters wide, and 13.5 meters high. If this is not possible, measure the size of your space and determine what fraction your space is when compared to the size of the ark.

Write the name of an animal on two separate pieces of paper. Repeat this until you have several pairs of animals. Plan for each child to have one piece of paper.

To begin the class, tell the children the size of the ark. Say, **Today, we are going to learn about Noah and the ark. The ark was huge! It was bigger than a soccer field! We will find out why it was so big.**

Distribute to each child a piece of paper with the name of an animal. Tell the children to read silently the name of the animal and to keep it a secret. If you have children who cannot read yet, whisper the name of the animal to them. When you give the signal, the children will make the sound of their animal and try to find their partner, the other child with the same animal name.

After the children have found their animal partner, if possible, take time to walk around the perimeter of the area to allow children to get an idea of how large the ark was. Tell the children what fraction your space is when compared to the ark.

## BIBLICAL LESSON

Prepare a Bible story based on the lesson's scripture verses. Children will understand the lesson better if you tell them the story rather than reading it to them.

After the story, encourage the children to discuss the story by asking the following questions. This will help them apply it to their lives. There may not be a right or wrong answer.

1. **How was Noah different from the other people?**

2. **How is your neighborhood similar or different from the place where Noah lived?**

3. **How would you react if God asked you to do something like building an ark?**

4. **Tell about a time when you thought you were the only person who wanted to do the right thing.**

Say, **It is difficult to do the right thing when no one else does it. Noah probably felt that way. Noah loved God and wanted to please him, but the other people did not care about God. Noah thought he was alone. Did God notice that Noah always tried to do the right thing? The Bible says that he did. God helped Noah to prepare for the flood, and all of Noah's family survived.**

**God does notice our efforts to love him and to do the right thing. We need to love and serve God regardless of the attitudes of other people.**

## MEMORY VERSE

Practice the study's memory verse. You will find suggestions for memory verse activities on pages 110.

## ADDITIONAL ACTIVITIES

Choose from these options to enhance the children's Bible study.

1. Study more about Noah's ark. Ask the children to draw an ark. Help them design space inside for the animals to live, the people to live, and other things like food and water storage.

2. Make a small model of the ark from papier-mâché or clay.

3. Write a drama about the conversations between Noah and his sons as they built the ark.

4. Play a game or do an activity in the following section that relates to this lesson (p. 49ff).

# BASIC QUESTIONS

1. *What had become great on the earth? (6:5)*
   1. **Man's wickedness**
   2. Man's goodness
   3. The Bible does not say.

2. *What kind of man was Noah? (6:9)*
   1. Righteous
   2. Blameless
   3. **Both answers are correct.**

3. *Why did God tell Noah to build an ark? (6:13-14)*
   1. **The Lord would destroy the people and the earth.**
   2. The Lord said a great earthquake was coming.
   3. Both answers are correct.

4. *Who did the Lord say could go on the ark with Noah? (6:18)*
   1. Noah's wife
   2. Noah's sons and their wives
   3. **Both answers are correct.**

5. *How did Noah find the animals to put on the ark? (6:20)*
   1. His sons went out and found all the animals.
   2. **The animals came to Noah.**
   3. The Lord sent all the animals to a river.

6. *How long did the Lord say it would rain? (7:4)*
   1. **For 40 days and 40 nights**
   2. For 7 days and 7 nights
   3. For two weeks

7. *How much of what the Lord commanded him did Noah do? (7:5)*
   1. **All of what God commanded**
   2. Some of what God commanded
   3. None of what God commanded

8. *How old was Noah when he entered the ark? (7:11, 13)*
   1. 500 years old
   2. **600 years old**
   3. 700 years old

9. *What happened on the day the rain started? (7:13-15)*
   1. Noah allowed some neighbors to go into the ark.
   2. The people asked for forgiveness from God.
   3. **Noah and his family entered the ark with the animals.**

10. *After the animals entered, who shut Noah in? (7:16)*
    1. Noah
    2. **The Lord**
    3. His sons

# LESSON 5

## Genesis 7:17–8:22
## The Waters Rose

**MEMORY VERSE:** "As long as the earth endures, seedtime and harvest, cold and heat, summer and winter, day and night will never cease." (Genesis 8:22)

**BIBLICAL TRUTH:** God will help you to do the things he asks.

## BIBLICAL COMMENTARY

The Flood is one of the most exciting and dramatic accounts in the Bible. The story gives valuable insight into how God interacts with people.

God created people in his image for the purpose of having a special and unique relationship with them. This relationship deteriorated quickly with the disobedience of Adam and Eve. As the generations of people began to fill the earth, so did the rebellion, violence and sin.

However, God still loved people. God was especially pleased with Noah. "Noah found favor in the eyes of the Lord." The interaction between Noah and God helps us to understand the power of obedience to God's instructions.

God's act of mercy to Noah and his family provides for us an insight about the nature of God. God created the world, and he had the authority to destroy it. Yet, because he highly values relationships, he saved the human race from being totally destroyed. This shows God's unfailing love and mercy.

## WORDS OF OUR FAITH

- **sovereign** -- the power to rule with no limitation. A sovereign king is not controlled by any other person or nation.
- **an altar** -- a structure built by people in the Old Testament to offer sacrifices to God. To offer a sacrifice was a way that people worshipped God. Today, some churches have altars so that people can have a special place to talk to God.
- **a sacrifice** -- something valuable that is offered to God. In Old Testament times, the sacrifice was usually an animal, some fruit, or some grain. In Romans 12:1-2, the Bible tells us that we can offer our lives to be used according to God's purposes.

## ACTIVITY

You will need these items for this activity:

- white paper or cardstock
- crayons

After you tell the story, gather children into groups of five. Remind the children of the main points of the story: **1) flood waters rose, 2) God remembered Noah, 3) the ark landed on Mount Ararat, 4) Noah sent out a dove to look for dry ground 5) Noah built an altar to worship God.**

Distribute five pieces of paper to each group. Ask children in each group to decide who will draw these images: water, Noah, mountain, dove, altar. (Note: an altar can be drawn as a cairn or neatly stacked rocks.)

When the children finish the drawings, instruct them to put the pictures in order and retell the story using their images. Each child may tell the part of the story he or she drew. If time permits, have children switch cards and tell the story again.

Say, **The rising waters must have frightened Noah and his family. But God did not forget his promise. He remembered Noah. When you are worried about something, know that God remembers you too!**

## BIBLICAL LESSON

Prepare a Bible story based on the lesson's scripture verses. Children will understand the lesson better if you tell them the story rather than reading it to them.

After the story, encourage the children to discuss the story by asking the following questions. This will help them apply it to their lives. There may not be a right or wrong answer.

1. **Noah and his family waited for 40 days while the flood waters rose. Then they waited 150 days more. Then they waited, and waited and waited for the waters to recede. Have you ever had to wait for something? How did that make you feel?**

2. **What do you think Noah and his family did while they waited inside of the ark?**

3. **After Noah left the ark, how did he thank God?**

4. **Name something for which you can thank God.**

5. **How does the memory verse, Genesis 8:22, relate to this story?**

Say, **There are many opportunities for adults to serve God. What can a child do? Children can learn from Noah that God does not require them to leave where they live to serve him and obey him. Noah did what God asked him to do. Think about Noah when you ask, "What can I do to serve God?"** Remind the children that the best way we can serve God is to obey him.

### MEMORY VERSE

Practice the study's memory verse. You will find suggestions for memory verse activities on pages 110.

### ADDITIONAL ACTIVITIES

Choose from these options to enhance the children's Bible study.

1. Research an altar. How did people use altars during Bible times? Find other scripture passages that talk about making an altar to God. Make a model of one.

2. Create a diorama of the ark resting on the mountains of Ararat.

3. Draw a picture of the ark and your favorite animal.

4. Play a game or do an activity in the following section that relates to this lesson (p. 49ff).

## BASIC QUESTIONS

1. *How long did the rains last? (7:17)*
   1. 40 weeks
   2. **40 days**
   3. 40 hours

2. *What happened when God sent the rains? (7:19-21)*
   1. Every living thing on the earth died.
   2. Water covered even the highest mountains.
   3. **Both answers are correct.**

3. *Who remained alive on the earth? (7:23)*
   1. Noah
   2. The people who were with Noah in the ark
   3. **Both answers are correct.**

4. *Where did the ark come to rest? (8:4)*
   1. **The mountains of Ararat**
   2. The mountain of God
   3. The Garden of Eden

5. *After the rain stopped, which bird did Noah send out first? (8:7)*
   1. **A raven**
   2. A dove
   3. A pigeon

6. *What did the dove bring back to Noah? (8:11)*
   1. A blade of grass
   2. An apple
   3. **A freshly plucked olive leaf**

7. *When did Noah remove the covering from the ark? (8:13)*
   1. As soon as it stopped raining
   2. **When the water had dried up from the earth**
   3. Both answers are correct.

8. *What did Noah do with the altar he built? (8:20)*
   1. **He sacrificed some clean animals and birds to the Lord.**
   2. He sacrificed some unclean animals to the Lord.
   3. He sacrificed olive trees and fruit to the Lord.

9. *What did the Lord say he would never do again? (8:21)*
   1. Destroy all living creatures
   2. Curse the ground because of man
   3. **Both answers are correct.**

10. *How long did God say that summer and winter would endure? (8:22)*
    1. Forever
    2. **As long as the earth endures**
    3. Until the next flood

# LESSON 6

## Genesis 9:1-20, 28-29
## The Rainbow in the Clouds

**MEMORY VERSE:** "I have set my rainbow in the clouds, and it will be the sign of the covenant between me and the earth." (Genesis 9:13)

**BIBLICAL TRUTH:** God established a covenant with people.

### BIBLICAL COMMENTARY

God confirms his covenant with Noah and honors Noah's obedience. God also initiates and honors a covenant with people. God maintains his covenant with humanity despite their unfaithfulness. The covenant between God, the earth, and its inhabitants is the final part of this dramatic story.

For the children to understand this resolution, it is important to understand what a covenant is. A covenant is a serious agreement between two people. In this case, the covenant is between God and the earth, the people, and all other life on the earth (the animals, the birds, and the fish). God said the rainbow was the sign of his covenant.

After the flood, God had different expectations for people. People are not restricted to a diet of fruit and vegetables. God allowed people also to eat the meat. However, God still put constraints on how his people should prepare the meat. For instance, they needed to drain the blood first. God still cares for people and he cares about how they live.

God does not tolerate sin. God will continue to work to make the world right. God does notice our efforts to serve him, and he honors those who obey him. Despite the wickedness of people, God still treasures those whom he created in his image.

### WORDS OF OUR FAITH

- **a covenant** -- a special, serious agreement between two people or between a person and God.

### ACTIVITY

You will need these items for this activity:

- six pieces of paper, each one colored with a color of the rainbow (red, orange, yellow, green, blue, purple).
- markers or crayons in the same colors
- a black marker or a crayon
- small pieces of paper, one for each child

To prepare, go to a large area and hide each colored sheet of paper in a different place, along with the matching color of marker or crayon. Choose one child to be the Rainbow Catcher, the player who tries to tag the other players and impede their progress.

To play, send out everyone except the Rainbow Catcher in search of the markers or crayons. Each time a child finds one of the markers or crayons, he or she should mark discreetly a stripe on his or her paper. The child should leave the marker or crayon in place. The Rainbow Catcher will try to tag the players. Every time he or she does, the Rainbow Catcher uses the black marker or crayon to eliminate one of the colored stripes on the paper of the child. The first player to get one stripe in each color wins.

Say, **That was a fun game, and it helped us to learn the colors of a rainbow. But, did you know there is more to a rainbow than just pretty colors? Today we will learn that God gave a special meaning to the rainbow.**

### BIBLICAL LESSON

Prepare a Bible story based on the lesson's scripture verses. Children will understand the lesson better if you tell them the story rather than reading it to them.

After the story, encourage the children to discuss the story by asking the following questions. This will help them apply it to their lives. There may not be a right or wrong answer.

1. What do you think of when you see a rainbow?

2. How long are you able to keep a promise to your family or your friends? Could you keep a promise for eternity? What makes it difficult to keep a promise?

3. Noah was 950 years old. What do you think it would be like to be 950 years old? What changes might happen during your life?

4. How does the memory verse, Genesis 9:13, relate to this story?

Say, **God's Word was true for the people in biblical times, and his Word is true for us today. God promised not to destroy the whole earth again with a flood. It was a promise to Noah, to his sons, and to all who came after them.**

**When we see a rainbow in the sky, we remember God's promise to us. It is a sign of the covenant that God made with Noah long ago. God keeps his promises.**

## MEMORY VERSE

Practice the study's memory verse. You will find suggestions for memory verse activities on pages 110.

## ADDITIONAL ACTIVITIES

Choose from these options to enhance the children's Bible study.

1. Discuss what a covenant is. A covenant can be a formal binding agreement that defines the relationships and the responsibilities between two or more people. There are four other major biblical covenants: the covenant with Abraham (Genesis 12); the covenant with Moses (Exodus 19 and 23); the covenant with David (2 Samuel 7); the new covenant (Luke 22:20). How are they alike? How are they different?

2. Ask the children to write letters to God, thanking him for keeping his covenant with people. Have the children include thanks to God for remembering his promise. If you have enough time and the children are interested, give them time to add some promises they will make to God also.

3. Play a game or do an activity in the following section that relates to this lesson (p. 49ff).

## BASIC QUESTIONS

1. *After he blessed them, what did God tell Noah and his sons to do? (9:1)*
   **1. Be fruitful and fill the earth.**
   2. Rename the animals.
   3. Do not sin anymore.

2. *What could people eat after the Flood? (9:3-4)*
   1. Green plants
   2. Meat with no lifeblood
   **3. Both answers are correct.**

3. *Why will God demand an accounting for the life of people? (9:5-6)*
   **1. Man is created in the image of God.**
   2. Animals are more important than people.
   3. The Bible does not say.

4. *What was the covenant that God made with all living creatures? (9:11)*
   **1. He will never again send a flood to destroy the earth and all life on it.**
   2. He will no longer punish the people.
   3. He will never destroy the earth with fire.

5. *What sign did God give for the covenant he made? (9:13)*
   **1. A rainbow**
   2. The ark
   3. Both answers are correct.

6. *How long did God say this covenant would last? (9:12)*
   1. As long as Noah lived
   **2. For all generations**
   3. As long as Noah's sons lived

7. *What will God remember when the rainbow appears? (9:16)*
   **1. The everlasting covenant he made**
   2. The need for rain on the earth
   3. Both answers are correct.

8. *From whom did all of the people come after the Flood? (9:19)*
   **1. Shem, Ham, and Japheth**
   2. The sons of Abraham
   3. Both answers are correct.

9. *For how many years did Noah live after the Flood? (9:28)*
   1. 950 years
   2. 150 years
   **3. 350 years**

10. *How old was Noah when he died? (9:29)*
    1. 450 years
    **2. 950 years**
    3. 1050 years

# LESSON 7

## Genesis 12:1-9; 13:5-18
## Calls and Choices

**MEMORY VERSE:** "By faith Abraham, when called to go to a place he would later receive as his inheritance, obeyed and went, even though he did not know where he was going." (Hebrews 11:8)

**BIBLICAL TRUTH:** You can trust God to do what he says.

### BIBLICAL COMMENTARY

Abram's relationship with God was different from Lot's relationship with God. Abram and Lot made different choices and this study shows the results of those choices.

Lot and Abram left Haran with their families. When the new land could not support both families, Abram was gracious and offered Lot the first choice of land. Abram did not protect his own interest. Rather, he trusted God to bring him to the Promised Land and he was generous to Lot.

People often make choices based on what they think is best for them. God wants people to trust him and to choose his way. We cannot see into the future. Many times, we do not realize how it is possible for choices that we make today to affect the world tomorrow and in future years. However, God knows. So we should trust and obey God.

This lesson is a great opportunity to highlight Abram's faith. Abram's faith will affect the lives of his son (Isaac), his grandsons (Esau and Jacob), and even his great-grandson (Joseph).

### ACTIVITY

You will need these items for this activity:
- 2 suitcases
- 2 sets of clothing (shirts, shoes)
- 2 sets of household items, to represent moving (pots, books, towels)
- 2 tables

- a stopwatch or a clock

Before class, arrange one suitcase, a set of clothing, and a set of household items on each table at the front of the room. The sets of clothing and household items should be equal in the quantity, the size, and the number of items. Provide enough items to make it a challenge to fit everything in the suitcases. Two children will race to find out who can be the first to pack everything in a suitcase.

Tell the children that you will give them 60 seconds to pack the suitcase. (It may take a longer time than this.) The goal is to be the first one to place everything in the suitcase and to close it. If time permits, let every child have an opportunity to pack a suitcase.

Say, **Today we will learn about some people who packed their belongings and moved to a new place. They had some tough decisions to make. We will learn how they responded to God's call to move.**

### BIBLICAL LESSON

Prepare a Bible story based on the lesson's scripture verses. Children will understand the lesson better if you tell them the story rather than reading it to them.

After the story, encourage the children to discuss the story by asking the following questions. This will help them apply it to their lives. There may not be a right or wrong answer.

1. **How would you respond if God asked you to leave your home and follow him? What would be the most difficult thing for you if God asked you to move?**

2. **Who do you think made a good choice in this story? Why?**

3. **Who do you think made a bad choice in this story? Why?**

4. What does it mean to trust God?

5. Discuss today's memory verse, Hebrews 11:8. What did it mean for Abram to leave Haran? Do you know the story of anyone who had to trust God in a difficult situation?

Say, **It can be difficult to make choices. Abram and Lot made some choices to settle the quarrels of their herdsmen. Out of respect for his uncle who was older, Lot should give Abram first choice. However, Lot chose first.**

**Abram gave up the first choice because he had faith in God. Abram trusted God to help him on his journey. Abram trusted God to provide for his needs. And, Abram trusted God to do what God said that he would do.**

## MEMORY VERSE

Practice the study's memory verse. You will find suggestions for memory verse activities on pages 110.

## ADDITIONAL ACTIVITIES

Choose from these options to enhance the children's Bible study.

1. Ask, **Have you ever moved to a new town? Write a story about your move. If you have not moved, pretend that you did. Include why you moved, what was easy and what was difficult about your move, and how you felt about it.**

2. Have the children draw a picture or make a scene that shows Lot and his herds on the plain of the Jordan River.

3. Play a game or do an activity in the following section that relates to this lesson (p. 49ff).

# BASIC QUESTIONS

1. *What did the Lord tell Abram to do? (12:1)*
   **1. To go to a land that the Lord would show him.**
   2. To move to the sea.
   3. To stay in the land of his father.

2. *Who went with Abram? (12:5)*
   1. Sarai and Lot
   2. The people of his household
   **3. Both answers are correct.**

3. *What did the Lord say that he would give to Abram's offspring? (12:6-7)*
   1. The land where no one lived
   **2. The land of Canaan**
   3. Both answers are correct.

4. *Who lived in the land God gave to Abram? (12:6-7)*
   **1. Canaanites**
   2. No one
   3. Abram's parents

5. *Why did the herdsmen of Abram and Lot quarrel? (13:6-7)*
   1. The land could not support both herds.
   2. Abram and Lot had many possessions.
   **3. Both answers are correct.**

6. *Why did Abram and Lot go to separate places? (13:8-9)*
   1. They did not like each other.
   **2. They did not want anyone to quarrel.**
   3. Lot wanted to return to Haran.

7. *Where did Lot choose to live? (13:10-12)*
   1. The well-watered plain of the Jordan
   2. Among the cities
   **3. Both answers are correct.**

8. *How does the Bible describe the men of Sodom? (13:13)*
   **1. They were wicked, and they sinned greatly against the Lord.**
   2. They were relatives of Abram.
   3. Both answers are correct.

9. *Where did Abram choose to live? (13:18)*
   1. The bank of the Jordan River
   **2. Near the great trees of Mamre in Hebron**
   3. Near the cities

10. *What did Abram do after he moved to Hebron? (13:18)*
    1. He visited Haran.
    **2. He built an altar to the Lord.**
    3. Both answers are correct.

# LESSON 8

## Genesis 15:1-21
## Promises and Covenants

**MEMORY VERSE:** "Do not be afraid, Abram. I am your shield, your very great reward." (Genesis 15:1b)

**BIBLICAL TRUTH:** God is worthy of our faith and trust in him.

### BIBLICAL COMMENTARY

Abram was a rich and a successful man. However, Abram lacked a son. God told Abram about a great reward, but Abram questioned how great it could be since he was childless. The Lord assured Abram that he would have a son. Abram trusted that God would keep his promise.

Once again, Abram questioned God about this promise. This time, God responded by making a covenant with Abram. Abram arranged the animals in a manner that was common for people who wanted to pledge an oath. Taking this oath was a serious commitment. In this ritual, two people met in the middle of the animal pieces in order to indicate that they both agreed to participate in the oath. In verse 17, God is represented by the firepot and the torch that passed through the pieces. Abram did not pass through the pieces, as he would have done in a normal covenant ceremony. God made the covenant, and Abram received it.

The Lord fulfilled His promise and gave Abram the descendants and the land. Despite Abram's questions, Genesis 15:6 described Abram's faith: "Abram believed the LORD, and he credited it to him as righteousness." As you teach this lesson, help the children to remember that they can trust the promises of God.

### WORDS OF OUR FAITH

- to be **righteous** -- to be in a right relationship with God and to obey him because of it.

- **descendants** -- the offspring (children, grandchildren, great-grandchildren, etc.) of a person. The descendants of Abram became known as the Israelites.

### ACTIVITY

You will need these items for this activity:

- copies of a simple covenant that you will make. You will need one for each child
- pens

Before class, make a simple covenant for each child. Provide a place to put a person's name, the dates, a description of some work to be done, and several lines for signatures. Make enough copies that the children have the opportunity to fill out more than one covenant.

Say, **God called Abram to leave his homeland and travel to an unknown place. God made a covenant with Abram that in the future God would give to him a son. God also promised to give to him all the land that he would show to him. What is a covenant?** (Allow time for the children to answer.) **What was unusual about the covenant that God made with Abram?** (Normally, both people in a covenant would pass through the pieces of animal, but in this covenant only God did that.)

**God was faithful to Abram and he guided him on his journey to Canaan. However, God did not complete his promise to Abram until after the covenant was complete.**

Pass out copies of the blank contracts to each child. Tell them to think of promises that people make to each other, such as the purchase of an object, or an agreement to do a job for a certain price.

Say, **Today, you will write some covenants. For example: Write a covenant with a friend or parent. Make a promise to do a specific task in your home or at your school for one month. Write your name, the date, and the task that you will do. Then sign your name and ask the other person to sign his or her name.** Instruct the children to give the contract to the other person and to fulfil the promise or covenant for one month. This will remind them of God's promises that he made to us and the promises we make to others.

## BIBLICAL LESSON

Prepare a Bible story based on the lesson's scripture verses. Children will understand the lesson better if you tell them the story rather than reading it to them.

After the story, encourage the children to discuss the story by asking the following questions. This will help them apply it to their lives. There may not be a right or wrong answer.

1.  **What situations cause you to doubt God's promises?**

2.  **Abram had no children at the time that God promised him descendants as numerous as the stars in the sky. How do you think Abram felt? Would you believe God if you were in Abram's place? Why?**

Say, **How difficult is it to wait for someone to fulfil a promise?** (Allow time for the children to respond.) **God made a covenant with Abram, and God showed Abram how he would fulfil that promise. God would provide an heir to inherit Abram's possessions, and he would give the Promised Land to them.**

**Genesis shows that we can trust God. God continues to show us that he is faithful to keep his promises.**

## MEMORY VERSE

Practice the study's memory verse. You will find suggestions for memory verse activities on pages 110.

## ADDITIONAL ACTIVITIES

Choose from these options to enhance the children's Bible study.

1.  Ask, **To whom does God refer in Genesis 15:13-16? What happened to them?** (This refers to God's people in Egypt. See Exodus 13:14-16.)

2.  The Bible uses the words offspring and descendants. These are the children, grand-children, great-grandchildren, etc. of a person. Write the name of one of the children's grandparents on the board. Then, help the child to write all the descendants.

3.  Play a game or do an activity in the following section that relates to this lesson (p. 49ff).

## BASIC QUESTIONS

1.  *Why did Abram think that his servant Eliezer would receive Abram's inheritance? (15:2)*
    1. Abram was not obedient to the Lord.
    **2. Abram did not have a child of his own.**
    3. Both answers are correct.

2.  *Whom did God say would be Abram's heir? (15:4)*
    1. Eliezer
    **2. A son from his own body**
    3. No one

3.  *Why did God take Abram outside? (15:5)*
    1. To show the heavens and the stars to him
    2. To show how many offspring that he would receive
    **3. Both answers are correct.**

4.  *What question did Abram ask the Lord about the land? (15:8)*
    **1. "How can I know that I will gain possession of it?"**
    2. "Why are the Canaanites still in the land?"
    3. "When will I have a son to help me?"

5.  *What did Abram do with the animals that he brought to the Lord? (15:10)*
    **1. He cut the larger animals in two and arranged the halves opposite each other.**
    2. He cut the birds in half.
    3. Both answers are correct.

6.  *When did the thick and dreadful darkness come over Abram? (15:12)*
    1. As the sun was rising
    **2. While Abram was in a deep sleep**
    3. Both answers are correct.

7.  *About whom did the Lord tell Abram? (15:13)*
    **1. His descendants**
    2. His servant, Eliezer
    3. Both answers are correct.

8.  *How long would Abram's descendants live in a country not their own? (15:13)*
    1. 40 years
    2. 100 years
    **3. 400 years**

9.  *How would that country treat Abram's descendants? (15:13)*
    **1. They will be enslaved and mistreated there.**
    2. They would be treated well.
    3. They would be treated like common people.

10. *When did the smoking firepot with a blazing torch appear? (15:17)*
    1. In the middle of the day
    **2. When the sun had set**
    3. The morning of the next day

# LESSON 9

## Genesis 21:1-6; 22:1-18
## Love Tested

**MEMORY VERSE:** "Because you have done this and have not withheld your son, your only son, I will surely bless you." (Genesis 22:16b-17a)

**BIBLICAL TRUTH:** God helps us to obey him in all situations.

## BIBLICAL COMMENTARY

God changed Abram's name in chapter 17 with the confirmation of the covenant. Abram is now Abraham. Chapter 21 tells of the anticipated son, Isaac, who is born to Sarai. Her name becomes Sarah.

The Lord tested Abraham's devotion. He asked Abraham to sacrifice Isaac as an offering of worship to God. Remember, Isaac is not only Abraham's beloved son, but also the means by which God intended to fulfil his promise to Abraham.

Genesis 22:8-12 tells about Abraham's journey which was very emotional for him. Abraham believed that God would provide a sacrifice. Second, Abraham intended to go through with the sacrifice. Finally, the Lord saw Abraham's complete devotion. He did not withhold anything from God, including his son, Isaac.

When God saw Abraham's great faith, he reassured Abraham of the blessings to come. God also promised that he would bless all nations because of Abraham's obedience. Abraham proved that God's faith in him was worthy of the covenant and the blessings he promised.

## WORDS OF OUR FAITH

- **trust** -- complete dependence on God and his promises; a belief that God will do what he says

## ACTIVITY

You will need these items for this activity:
- a stopwatch or clock
- samples of some items that are important to children
- a piece of paper for each child
- pens or pencils

Before class, arrange on a table the items that are important to children. These are items that the children could sacrifice for a week to show their love for God. Provide a large variety of items. These items will represent things that children could sacrifice.

Say, **In today's lesson, God fulfilled his covenant to Abraham when he gave Abraham the promised son. Abraham faithfully trusted God. Have you ever waited for a long time for someone to fulfil a promise?**

**God tested Abraham when he asked Abraham to sacrifice his son. Abraham showed his love for God by his willingness to do what God asked.**

Point out some of the items on the table. Ask, **Which of these items would be special to you?** (Let the children respond.) **What if God asked you to show him how much you loved him? Would you give up something that was very important to you? What would you do?**

Give each child a piece of paper, and encourage the children to write a poem or draw a picture that reveals how it feels to sacrifice something for God.

## BIBLICAL LESSON

Prepare a Bible story based on the lesson's scripture verses. Children will understand the lesson better if you tell them the story rather than reading it to them.

After the story, encourage the children to discuss the story by asking the following questions. This will help them apply it to their lives. There may not be a right or wrong answer.

1. **What do Abraham's actions tell us about his faith in God?**

2. **What does Abraham's faith teach us about what God wants from us?**

3. **What would be the most difficult thing for you to sacrifice?**

Say, **Abraham waited for many years for a son. After the birth of Isaac, God asked Abraham to sacrifice Isaac.** If the children are concerned about God asking someone to sacrifice a child, tell them that this was a special event. It was the only time God asked someone to do this. **Abraham could not understand what God planned to do, but he obeyed God completely. As a result, God promised to bless Abraham and his family.**

**God wants us to have the same kind of faith and the same kind of trust in him.**

## MEMORY VERSE

Practice the study's memory verse. You will find suggestions for memory verse activities on pages 110.

## ADDITIONAL ACTIVITIES

Choose from these options to enhance the children's Bible study.

1. Help the children to compare and to contrast the sacrifice Abraham made with the sacrifice God made for us.

2. Write a journal entry for Abraham for the previous day and the day that followed the sacrifice on the mountain.

3. Play a game or do an activity in the following section that relates to this lesson (p. 49ff).

# BASIC QUESTIONS

1. *What happened at the very time that God promised? (21:2)*
   **1. Abraham and Sarah had a son.**
   2. The Canaanites left the area.
   3. Both answers are correct.

2. *What did Abraham and Sarah name their son? (21:4)*
   1. Abimelech
   2. David
   **3. Isaac**

3. *Where did God ask Abraham to take Isaac? (22:2)*
   1. To visit Lot
   **2. To the region of Moriah**
   3. To Haran

4. *What did God ask Abraham to do in Moriah? (22:2)*
   **1. To sacrifice Isaac**
   2. To meet with the Canaanites
   3. Both answers are correct.

5. *Who went with Abraham to Moriah? (22:3)*
   1. Isaac
   2. Two servants
   **3. Both answers are correct.**

6. *Who asked, "Where is the lamb for the burnt offering?" (22:7)*
   1. Abraham
   **2. Isaac**
   3. The servants

7. *What happened to Isaac after Abraham built the altar? (22:9)*
   1. Isaac ran away from Abraham.
   2. Isaac sat down, and he refused to move.
   **3. Abraham bound Isaac, and he placed Isaac on the altar.**

8. *Who stopped Abraham before he sacrificed Isaac? (22:11-12)*
   1. The servants
   **2. The angel of the Lord**
   3. Sarah

9. *What did the Lord provide for the sacrifice? (22:13)*
   **1. A ram**
   2. A goat
   3. A donkey

10. *What did the angel of the Lord say about Abraham's willingness to sacrifice his son? (22:16-17)*
    1. God would bless Abraham.
    2. Abraham would have many descendants.
    **3. Both answers are correct.**

# LESSON 10

## Genesis 24:1-4, 10-21, 28-33, 50-54, 61-67
## Here Comes the Bride

**MEMORY VERSE:** "I will instruct you and teach you in the way you should go; I will counsel you with my loving eye on you." (Psalm 32:8)

**BIBLICAL TRUTH:** God cares about our lives and leads us as we follow him.

### BIBLICAL COMMENTARY

God's covenant with Abraham continued through Isaac. It was the highest priority. It was important that Isaac find the right wife to continue God's promise of many descendants for Abraham. This would enable Isaac to fulfil his role in God's covenant.

God's guidance influenced Rebekah and her family. They responded positively to the question, "Will Rebekah go with this man?" Each person had a choice to make. Would they trust God? We do not know the motivation of each person. However, the Bible does indicate that each person was obedient in the steps that led to the marriage of Rebekah and Isaac.

Children learn from this passage that God is concerned with their everyday life, and that God wants to help them make the right choices.

### ACTIVITY

Play a game of "Teacher, may I?" To begin the game, the teacher stands at one end of a room while all of the children form a line at the other end. The children take turns and ask "Teacher, may I?" and make a movement suggestion. For example, one child asks, "Teacher, may I take five giant steps forward?" The leader either replies "Yes, you may" or "No, you may not do that, but you may take five small steps instead." The teacher inserts his or her own suggestion. The children usually move closer to the leader but sometimes the teacher's instructions lead the children farther away. Even if the leader makes an unfavorable suggestion, the child must perform it. The first child to reach the leader wins the game.

Some suggestions for movements include:

- Take 3 steps forward. (Use any number.)
- Take 2 steps backward. (Use any number.)
- Take 5 giant steps forward. (This is usually a small number because of the large size of the step.)
- Take 12 baby steps forward. (This is usually a large number because of the small size of the step.)
- Hop forward 5 times like a frog. (Use any number.)
- Run forward while you count to five. (Use any number.)

Play the game again, if time allows.

Say, **In this game, you asked the leader's permission, and you made the choice to follow the leader. You did this even if the leader's will was not your will.**

**In today's story, we will learn how several people made choices that were in God's will.**

### BIBLICAL LESSON

Prepare a Bible story based on the lesson's scripture verses. Children will understand the lesson better if you tell them the story rather than reading it to them.

After the story, encourage the children to discuss the story by asking the following questions. This will help them apply it to their lives. There may not be a right or wrong answer.

1. **Have you ever waited a long time to get something that you wanted? Was it worth the wait?**

2. **Why was it important for God to provide a wife for Isaac?**

3. **Who made a good choice in this story and what was the choice?** (There could be more than one good answer.)

4. **How does the memory verse, Psalm 32:8, relate to this story?**

Say, **God cared about Abraham, Isaac and Rebekah. God also cares about your life. You can ask God to help you make right choices. One of the things that you learned in Genesis is that God is faithful and that God keeps his promises. God knows you, and he knows your needs. When you make a choice, you can ask God to help you make the right choice.**

## MEMORY VERSE

Practice the study's memory verse. You will find suggestions for memory verse activities on page 110.

## ADDITIONAL ACTIVITIES

Choose from these options to enhance the children's Bible study.

1. Say, **Pretend that you are Rebekah. Write a diary entry that tells how you felt when you met the servant and he gave you those expensive gifts. How would you feel about going to a different land to marry a stranger? Pretend you are the servant. What were your thoughts and reactions?**

2. Research Old Testament wedding customs or talk about how wedding customs changed in your country.

3. Compare a wedding today in your town with the wedding of Rebekah. How are they alike? How are they different?

4. Play a game or do an activity in the following section that relates to this lesson (p. 49ff).

# BASIC QUESTIONS

1. *Why did Abraham send his chief servant to his relatives? (24:4)*
   1. To bring back his father to him
   2. **To find a wife for his son, Isaac**
   3. To worship in his homeland

2. *For what did the servant pray when he reached the well at Nahor? (24:11-12)*
   1. **Success**
   2. Rest for the camels
   3. Both answers are correct.

3. *Why did the servant ask Rebekah for some water? (24:13-14)*
   1. **He wanted to determine if she was the woman whom God chose for Isaac.**
   2. She was the only one who spoke his language.
   3. She was the only one at the well.

4. *Why did Laban hurry out to the well to meet the servant? (24:28-31)*
   1. Rebekah ran home, and she told her family what happened.
   2. Laban prepared the house for him and a place for his camels.
   3. **Both answers are correct.**

5. *What did Laban and Bethuel say after the servant explained why he came? (24:50)*
   1. **"This is from the LORD."**
   2. "We will not let Rebekah go with you."
   3. Both answers are correct.

6. *What did the servant give Rebekah and her family? (24:53)*
   1. Gold and silver jewelry
   2. Clothing and costly gifts
   3. **Both answers are correct.**

7. *When did Rebekah leave with the servant? (24:54)*
   1. A week later
   2. **The next morning**
   3. Ten days later

8. *Where was Isaac when Rebekah saw him? (24:63-64)*
   1. **In the field, meditating**
   2. In his tent, eating
   3. By the river, fishing

9. *What did the servant do when he saw Isaac? (24:66)*
   1. He prayed to God.
   2. **He told Isaac everything that he did.**
   3. Both answers are correct.

10. *How did Isaac feel after he married Rebekah? (24:67)*
    1. He loved Rebekah.
    2. She comforted him after his mother's death.
    3. **Both answers are correct.**

# LESSON 11

## Genesis 25:5-11, 19-34
## It's Twins!

**MEMORY VERSE:** "Even small children are known by their actions, so is their conduct really pure and up right?" (Proverbs 20:11)

**BIBLICAL TRUTH:** God works in our lives, even when we encounter conflict.

## BIBLICAL COMMENTARY

Chapter 25, and the chapters that follow it, develop two major themes. The first is how one generation passed the covenant to the next. The second is the struggle between two brothers. After Abraham died, God blessed Isaac who became the next generation's heir. Esau was the next in line to become the heir to the family and God's covenant. Because of the shrewdness of Jacob, Esau flippantly sold his future for a lunch (25:34).

Family dynamics and relationships are the major themes of this study. This family encounters death, births, deceit, favoritism, power struggles, broken relationships, and hints of marital discord. As we follow this family's story, sometimes God will appear in the forefront, and, at other times, in the background. But, he worked with this family, even though at times they were dysfunctional.

## WORDS OF OUR FAITH

- a **promise** -- a statement that someone will do something. In the Bible, God made promises. He always kept his promises.
- an **oath** -- a strong promise where someone asks God to witness the oath and to judge a person if her or she breaks it.
- the **birthright** -- the privilege that belongs to the firstborn son of a family. It meant the eldest son received influence and a double portion of inheritance after his father's death. The eldest son would be the next leader of the family.

## ACTIVITY

You will need these items for this activity:
- a sheet of paper
- a bowl
- a spoon

Before class, cut the paper into five pieces. Cut each piece of paper into a unique shape to represent a piece of meat. Write one of the questions below on each shape. Do not write the answers. You may write additional questions. Hide the pieces of paper around the room.

1. **Did Esau and Jacob often compete with each other?** (Yes, even before they were born)
2. **Who became Isaac's favorite son?** (Esau)
3. **Who became Rebekah's favorite son?** (Jacob)
4. **What are some issues that cause brothers or sisters to fight?** (Allow time for the children to respond.)
5. **How did Jacob trick Esau?** (He convinced Esau to sell his birthright for some stew.)

Say, **In the room are some pieces of paper that have the shape of a piece of meat. Each one has a question on it. Find these pieces of paper, and place them in this bowl.**

After the children find the pieces of paper, select a volunteer to stir the bowl with the spoon. Let a volunteer choose one question to answer. Repeat this with all the questions. If the children are unfamiliar with this story, complete this activity after you read the Bible story. You may combine the activity questions with the questions in the next section.

## BIBLICAL LESSON

Prepare a Bible story based on the lesson's scripture verses. Children will understand the lesson better if you tell them the story rather than reading it to them.

After the story, encourage the children to discuss the story by asking the following questions. This will help them apply it to their lives. There may not be a right or wrong answer.

1. **In your opinion, what was it like for Jacob to know that Esau was Isaac's favorite?**

2. **In your opinion, what was it like for Esau to know that Jacob was Rebekah's favorite?**

3. **What are some characteristics of Jacob?**

4. **How do you feel when your brother, sister, or friend cheats you?**

Say, **God kept his promise to Isaac. He blessed Rebekah with two sons instead of one. However, the two sons fought and competed with each other. Jacob even took advantage of his older brother so that he could obtain the birthright. Esau sold his birthright for a bowl of stew.**

**This story happened in Old Testament times. However, family problems still happen today. God is still faithful, even when members of a family struggle. God always keeps his promise to be with us and help us in difficult situations.**

## MEMORY VERSE

Practice the study's memory verse. You will find suggestions for memory verse activities on pages 110.

## ADDITIONAL ACTIVITIES

Choose from these options to enhance the children's Bible study.

1. Select two volunteers from the class. Have the first volunteer portray Esau. Have the second volunteer portray Jacob. Tell the children to dramatize the sale of Esau's birthright to Jacob.

2. Allow the children to share ways that God helped their family. Make a list of these stories. Use this list to show the children that God keeps his promises today.

3. Play a game or do an activity in the following section that relates to this lesson (p. 49ff).

## BASIC QUESTIONS

1. *What happened when Abraham died? (25:8-10)*
   1. Isaac moved to the land of Rebekah's family.
   2. **Ishmael and Isaac buried Abraham with Sarah.**
   3. Both answers are correct.

2. *Why did Isaac pray to the Lord for Rebekah? (25:21)*
   1. **She could not have children.**
   2. She wanted to see her family.
   3. Both answers are correct.

3. *What did the Lord tell Rebekah about her babies? (25:23)*
   1. They would live separate lives.
   2. The older would serve the younger.
   3. **Both answers are correct.**

4. *What were the names of Rebekah's twin boys? (25:24-26)*
   1. Isaac and Laban
   2. Isaac and Esau
   3. **Esau and Jacob**

5. *Which of these statements is true of Esau? (25:27)*
   1. He was a farmer who liked the fields.
   2. **He was a skillful hunter who liked the open country.**
   3. He was quiet and liked to stay among the tents.

6. *Which of these statements is true of Jacob? (25:27)*
   1. **He was quiet, and he liked to stay among the tents.**
   2. He was a fisherman who liked the river.
   3. He was a skillful hunter who liked the open country.

7. *When did Jacob say to Esau, "First, sell me your birthright"? (25:29-31)*
   1. After Esau came home famished
   2. After Esau asked Jacob for some stew
   3. **Both answers are correct.**

8. *Why did Esau say he was about to die? (25:30, 32)*
   1. He was wounded.
   2. **He was hungry.**
   3. He was sick.

9. *How did Esau sell his birthright to Jacob? (25:33)*
   1. **He swore an oath.**
   2. He signed a paper.
   3. He made a pile of stones.

10. *What did Esau despise? (25:34)*
    1. The life of a hunter
    2. The food he ate
    3. **His birthright**

# LESSON 12

## Genesis 27:1-41
## Deceived!

**MEMORY VERSE:** "Whoever of you loves life and desires to see many good days, keep your tongue from evil and your lips from telling lies." (Psalm 34:12-13)

**BIBLICAL TRUTH:** God allows us to make choices.

### BIBLICAL COMMENTARY

What happened to Isaac's family? They had a lot of problems. There were disagreements with neighbors about wells. Isaac lied to the king of the Philistines and said that Rebekah was his sister, not his wife. Esau married two Hittite women who were "a source of grief to Isaac and Rebekah." The family was deceitful and selfish. Rebekah took advantage of Isaac's blindness to advance Jacob instead of Esau.

The way that Jacob received his blessing was another deception. Jacob gained material possessions through the birthright of Esau. Jacob then gained the spiritual blessings of God through the blessing of Isaac.

Abraham's family had many problems that involved betrayal between husband and wife and between brothers. The betrayal resulted in Esau's plot to murder Jacob. Isaac and Rebekah sent Jacob to the homeland of Rebekah. This separated the family.

In this passage, there are many examples of people who made wrong choices. God did not intervene in Jacob's deception of Esau. However, God is not weak and people cannot manipulate him. God chooses to give us freedom to make choices, and he allows us to suffer the consequences. In future studies, the children will learn how God worked with Jacob to achieve God's purposes.

### WORDS OF OUR FAITH

- **free will** -- the ability and the freedom to make choices. God gives free will to everyone.

- the **blessing** -- a covenant that God established between himself and Abraham. Abraham passed it to Isaac, who was the recognized heir of Abraham.

Jacob deceived his father and brother. As a result, Isaac passed the blessing to Jacob.

### ACTIVITY

You will need these items for this activity:

- a piece of cloth for a blindfold

Choose one of the children as a volunteer. Ask him or her to sit in the middle of the classroom. Place the blindfold over the child's eyes.

Say, **Isaac was blind. Rebekah and Jacob took advantage of the blindness of Isaac. Today, our volunteer will try to recognize people without the use of his or her eyes.**

Tell one of the children to sit across from the child with the blindfold. The child with the blindfold may feel the arms or the face of the child. Then, ask the child with the blindfold to guess who the other child is. Repeat this with all of the other students. Use a pencil and paper to record the number of guesses that the child makes.

Say, **We are often unable to tell if a choice is right or wrong. Even when we have evidence, we may still make the wrong choice.**

Say, **We will repeat this activity. Now we will do it differently. If the child with the blindfold is unable to decide who is in front of him or her after two guesses, the child may ask one person. That person will tell who is in front of the guesser.**

Choose a child to give the answers to the child with the blindfold. Repeat the activity, but use only two children this time. Place a child in front of the child with the blindfold. Let the child make two guesses orally. If the guesses are wrong, let the designated child tell who the child is.

Say, **When we have difficult choices to make, we need help. It is important to ask God for help with these choices. He will help us when we ask him.**

## BIBLICAL LESSON

Prepare a Bible story based on the les- son's scripture verses. Children will understand the lesson better if you tell them the story rather than reading it to them.

After the story, encourage the children to discuss the story by asking the following questions. This will help them apply it to their lives. There may not be a right or wrong answer.

1. Rebekah planned for Jacob to steal Esau's blessing. Why did Jacob agree to participate?

2. Sometimes, our friends encourage us to do things that are wrong. What do you say to your friends when this happens?

3. Jacob deceived Isaac. Has anyone deceived you? How did you feel?

4. Esau wanted to kill Jacob for what Jacob did. When someone does something wrong to you, how do you react? Is it easy to forgive others? Where do you find the strength to forgive?

Say, **We have studied an amazing Bible story. It had elements of trickery and deceit. We have learned that God allows us to make choices. Those choices affect our future. Jacob made a bad choice that had a permanent effect. However, God stayed faithful to his covenant.**

**Today, God allows us to make choices. These choices will affect our futures.**

## MEMORY VERSE

Practice the study's memory verse. You will find suggestions for memory verse activities on pages 110.

## ADDITIONAL ACTIVITIES

Choose from these options to enhance the children's Bible study.

1. As a class, make a list of choices that the children will face. These choices may be temptations they experience at home, at school, or with their friends. For each choice, discuss what the future consequences may be for each decision.

2. Say, **Jacob chose to participate in Rebekah's plan to deceive Isaac. Imagine that Jacob decided not to participate. What are some possible consequences of this decision? What would be different in this story?**

3. Play a game or do an activity in the following section that relates to this lesson (p. 49ff).

# BASIC QUESTIONS

1. *What did Isaac ask Esau to do? (27:3-4)*
   1. To dig a new well
   2. To ask Jacob to bring him a goat
   3. **To hunt some wild game and to prepare a meal for him**

2. *What did Isaac want to give Esau? (27:6-7)*
   1. Some food
   2. **His blessing**
   3. New clothes

3. *What did Rebekah do after she overheard the words of Esau and Isaac? (27:8-10)*
   1. **She told Jacob to serve Isaac a meal.**
   2. She helped Esau prepare the food that he brought.
   3. Both answers are correct.

4. *How did Rebekah and Jacob trick Isaac? (27:15-17)*
   1. They made Isaac think that Jacob was Esau.
   2. They served Isaac the meal while Esau hunted wild animals.
   3. **Both of the answers are correct.**

5. *What did Isaac say when he touched Jacob? (27:22)*
   1. "The voice is the voice of Esau."
   2. **"The voice is the voice of Jacob."**
   3. "The hands are the hands of Jacob."

6. *What happened when Esau returned from his hunt? (27:30-31)*
   1. **He also prepared a meal to serve to Isaac.**
   2. Jacob blessed Esau.
   3. Both answers are correct.

7. *Why did Isaac tremble violently? (27:33, 35-36)*
   1. **He realized he had blessed Jacob.**
   2. The food made him sick.
   3. He lost his ability to see.

8. *How did Jacob deceive Esau? (27:36)*
   1. He took Esau's birthright.
   2. He took Esau's blessing.
   3. **Both answers are correct.**

9. *Where did Isaac say that Esau would dwell? (27:39)*
   1. Away from the earth's richness
   2. Away from the dew of heaven above
   3. **Both answers are correct**

10. *When did Esau plan to kill Jacob? (27:41)*
    1. The next morning
    2. When Jacob forgot what he did
    3. **After Isaac died**

31

# LESSON 13

## Genesis 28:10-22; 29:14b-30
## A Fresh Start

**MEMORY VERSE:** "I am the God of your father Abraham. Do not be afraid, for I am with you." (Genesis 26:24b)

**BIBLICAL TRUTH:** God works in our lives, even when we encounter conflict.

## BIBLICAL COMMENTARY

Rebekah told Jacob to flee from Esau. Jacob went to Haran, his mother's homeland, to live with Laban, the brother of Rebekah.

While Jacob travelled, he encountered the Lord. The Lord confirmed that he would bless him, even though Jacob deceived his brother to get the blessing. This was the same blessing that God gave to Abraham and to Isaac.

Jacob safely arrived at his destination, and Laban welcomed him. At first, the relationship between Laban and Jacob was good. Jacob exchanged his work for the privilege of marrying Rachel, the daughter of Laban.

Like Jacob, Laban was someone who deceived others. Laban secretly substituted Leah for Rachel as the bride. Jacob agreed to work seven more years for Rachel.

In spite of Jacob's failures, God honored his covenant to Jacob. This study shows God's ability to accomplish his purposes, despite the choices of people.

## WORDS OF OUR FAITH

- **choices** -- what we decide to do in a situation. We make right choices when we obey God. We make wrong choices when we disobey God.

- **worship** -- honor, reverence, or adoration for God. When we worship God, we declare that God is the ruler of our lives.

- **descendants** -- children who are born to a person or his children.

## ACTIVITY

You will need these items for this activity:

- a large stone
- several small pieces of paper
- some markers, pencils, or crayons
- some tape

Before class, place the stone in the middle of the room. If possible, place it in an upright position.

Say, **Jacob placed a stone in Bethel as a reminder of his conversation with God. In the conversation, God told Jacob that he will watch over Jacob wherever he went.**

**God watches over us too. Think about a time when you needed something and God provided it for you or your family. Write briefly on a piece of paper what God provided. We will attach these papers to our stone and say "Thank you" to God.**

After the children have attached their papers, let volunteers share what they wrote. Say, **This stone is a reminder of all of the things that God provided for us. God is faithful to us even though we sometimes disappoint him. He provides for us, and he speaks to us. We will learn more about a special time when God spoke to Jacob.**

## BIBLICAL LESSON

Prepare a Bible story based on the lesson's scripture verses. Children will understand the lesson better if you tell them the story rather than reading it to them.

After the story, encourage the children to discuss the story by asking the following questions. This will help them apply it to their lives. There may not be a right or wrong answer.

1. A monument helps us to remember something or someone who is important. Jacob used a stone as a monument to remember God's provision for him. What are some other ways we can remember how God provided for us?

2. How did Jacob feel when Laban deceived him? How could the deception of Laban make Jacob feel about the way he treated Esau?

3. God spoke to Jacob by using a dream. How does God speak to people today? How can we learn to listen to God?

Say, **God used a dream to communicate with Jacob. In the dream, God told Jacob that all of God's promises would happen. Jacob promised God that he would worship him, and he would give one-tenth of everything he owned to God.**

How does God send messages to us today? He may use a voice within us, the Bible, a song, a lesson, a sermon, or friendships with other Christians. There are other ways that God can speak to us. We must learn to listen to what God wants to tell us.

## MEMORY VERSE

Practice the study's memory verse. You will find suggestions for memory verse activities on pages 110.

## ADDITIONAL ACTIVITIES

Choose from these options to enhance the children's Bible study.

1. Say, **Jacob saw a ladder that led from earth to heaven. What do you think this ladder looked like? As a class, draw a picture of the ladder. Ask for suggestions from the class.**

2. Say, **Jacob worked for Laban for 14 years, so that he could marry Rachel. Was this a wise thing for him to do? Why? Think of something you want very much. Are you willing to work hard to obtain it? Why?**

3. Play a game or do an activity in the following section that relates to this lesson (p. 49ff).

# BASIC QUESTIONS

1. *Where did Jacob see the stairway? (28:10-12)*
   1. On the way to Haran
   2. In his dream
   **3. Both answers are correct.**

2. *Who spoke to Jacob in his dream? (28:12-13)*
   1. Rebekah
   **2. The Lord**
   3. Esau

3. *Whom did God say would be like the dust of the earth? (28:14)*
   **1. Jacob's descendants**
   2. Jacob's enemies
   3. Jacob's friends

4. *What did Jacob do after he awoke? (28:20)*
   1. He turned around and went home.
   **2. He made a vow to God.**
   3. Both answers are correct.

5. *What did Jacob ask God to do? (28:20)*
   1. To be with him and to watch over him
   2. To give him food to eat and clothes to wear
   **3. Both answers are correct.**

6. *With whom did Jacob stay in Haran? (29:14)*
   1. Esau
   **2. Laban**
   3. Rebekah

7. *Whom did Jacob want to marry? (29:18)*
   **1. Rachel**
   2. Leah
   3. Zilpah

8. *Whom did Laban give first to Jacob to marry? (29:23)*
   1. Bilhah
   2. Rachel
   **3. Leah**

9. *For how many more years did Jacob work for Rachel? (29:27)*
   1. 7 more years
   2. 2 more years
   3. 5 more years

10. *Whom did Jacob love more? (29:30)*
    1. Leah
    **2. Rachel**
    3. Bilhah

# LESSON 14

## Genesis 37:1-36
## Danger and the Dreamer

**MEMORY VERSE:** "The LORD is close to the brokenhearted and saves those who are crushed in spirit. A righteous person may have many troubles, but the LORD delivers him from them all." (Psalm 34:18-19)

**BIBLICAL TRUTH:** God allows people to make choices, and people are responsible for those choices.

## BIBLICAL COMMENTARY

In Studies 12 and 13, we learned about the deceit of Jacob. In this study, we will learn about the negative consequences of his actions.

Genesis 29—37 tells about the life of Jacob: his tense relationship with Laban, his wealth, and his reunion with Esau. He married two sisters, and he fathered eleven sons by four women. After their struggle, the Lord changed Jacob's name to Israel.

Jacob made many mistakes. He cheated Esau (27:36), and Laban cheated him (29:25). Jacob lied to Isaac (27:19), and Jacob believed a lie that his sons told him (37:32).

Jacob's marriages to Rachel and Leah caused the tension between the siblings. Jacob loved Rachel more than Leah. Jacob's favoritism of Joseph made his other sons angry. God honored his promise to Jacob, but Jacob was not as faithful as his grandfather, Abraham.

Help the children to understand that sibling rivalry and deception have negative effects. Negative consequences of bad choices cannot be altered, but people can learn from their mistakes and the mistakes of others.

## WORDS OF OUR FAITH

- to **mourn** -- to show sadness, usually when someone dies. It also means to feel great sorrow for personal sins and for all the sin and evil in the world.
- **the twelve tribes of Israel** -- The 12 sons of Israel (Jacob) were the ancestors for the people of Israel: Reuben, Simeon, Levi, Judah, Dan, Naphtali, Gad, Asher, Issachar, Zebulun, Joseph and Benjamin. Levi's tribe was special, and served God's temple.

Joseph's descendants were divided into the two tribes of his sons, Ephraim and Manasseh.

- a **cistern** -- a deep pit for storing water.
- a **shekel** -- a unit of weight, approximately 10 grams. Joseph's brother sold him into slavery for 20 silver shekel.

## ACTIVITY

You will need these items for this activity:

- a small table
- two chairs

Before class, set the table in the middle of the room, with the two chairs on opposite sides.

Divide the class into two teams. Say, **Now, we will play a game. Each team will send one person to the table. Place both of your hands on the table. I will ask a question. If you know the answer, raise your hand. The first person who raises his or her hand may answer the question. If the answer is correct, then that team gets a point.**

**Then two new players will sit at the table, and they will receive a new question. We will play until we answer all of the questions. At the end of the game, the team with the highest score wins!**

Use the following questions. You may create more questions if you need them.

1. **What would it be like to have many brothers who hate you?** (Accept any reasonable answer.)

2. **Why did Joseph's brothers hate him?** (He was their father's favorite son.)

3. **What did Joseph's dreams mean?** (One day Joseph would rule over his father and brothers.)

4. **What did Joseph's brothers do to him?** (They sold him to Ishmaelite or Midianite merchants who took him to Egypt.)

5. **How did Jacob's sons deceive him?** (They made him believe that an animal killed Joseph.)

## BIBLICAL LESSON

Prepare a Bible story based on the lesson's scripture verses. Children will understand the lesson better if you tell them the story rather than reading it to them.

After the story, encourage the children to discuss the story by asking the following questions. This will help them apply it to their lives. There may not be a right or wrong answer.

1. **Why were Joseph's brothers jealous of him? Have you ever felt jealous of one of your friends? How did you act toward that person?**

2. **How did Joseph feel about his dreams? Did Joseph boast to his brothers? Have you ever boasted to someone? Do you like to hear someone boast?**

3. **Joseph's brothers mistreated Joseph. Have you been mistreated by your family or friends? How did you respond?**

4. **Jacob was very sad when he thought Joseph was dead. How did you feel when you lost something or someone who is precious to you?**

Say, **Jacob deceived Esau and disobeyed God. Joseph's brothers did evil against Joseph. Then, Joseph's brothers deceived Jacob.**

**God allows us the freedom to make choices. However, our choices affect us and others. What you say and do today may affect you as an adult. Those choices may also affect your children.**

## MEMORY VERSE

Practice the study's memory verse. You will find suggestions for memory verse activities on pages 110.

## ADDITIONAL ACTIVITIES

Choose from these options to enhance the children's Bible study.

1. Ask the children to use crayons or markers and paper to illustrate Joseph's dreams. Let the children show these illustrations to the class.

2. Say, **Imagine that the brothers decided not to sell Joseph to the merchants. How would Joseph react to his brothers after he came out of the cistern?**

3. Use strips of colored paper to recreate Joseph's ornamented robe. Tape the strips of paper to the wall to create a picture of the robe.

4. Play a game or do an activity in the following section that relates to this lesson (p. 49ff).

## BASIC QUESTIONS

*1. Why did Joseph's brothers hate him? (37:3-4)*
   1. Jacob loved Joseph more than he loved his other sons.
   2. Joseph was born to Jacob in his old age
   **3. Both answers are correct.**

*2. What caused Joseph's brothers to hate him even more? (37:5-8)*
   **1. Joseph told them about his dream.**
   2. Joseph never worked with them.
   3. They hated him without a reason.

*3. Why did Joseph go to Shechem? (37:13-14)*
   1. To check on his brothers
   2. To bring back word about his brothers to Jacob
   **3. Both answers are correct.**

*4. What did the brothers want to do to Joseph? (37:19-20)*
   1. To leave him with all the flocks
   **2. To kill him and throw him into a cistern**
   3. To send him home to his father

*5. Who tried to rescue Joseph? (37:21-22)*
   1. The Lord
   2. Jacob
   **3. Reuben**

*6. What did Joseph's brothers take from him? (37:23)*
   1. His staff
   **2. His robe**
   3. His sandals

*7. Who came while Joseph's brothers ate their meal? (37:25)*
   **1. A caravan of Ishmaelites**
   2. Judah
   3. Jacob

*8. Where was the caravan going? (37:25)*
   1. To Dothan
   **2. To Egypt**
   3. To Shechem

*9. What did the brothers do when the Ishmaelite merchants came? (37:28)*
   1. They pulled Joseph out of the cistern.
   2. They sold Joseph for 20 shekels of silver.
   **3. Both answers are correct.**

*10. What happened when Joseph's brothers showed the robe to Jacob? (37:34-35)*
   **1. Jacob mourned for Joseph and would not be comforted.**
   2. Jacob asked if they lied.
   3. Both answers are correct.

# LESSON 15

## Genesis 40:1-23
## Faithful And Not Forgotten

**MEMORY VERSE:** "For the LORD gives wisdom; from his mouth come knowledge and understanding." (Proverbs 2:6)

**BIBLICAL TRUTH:** God does not abandon us in the midst of difficult times in our lives.

### BIBLICAL COMMENTARY

In Egypt, Joseph became a slave in the house of Potiphar. While Joseph was there, Potiphar wrongfully sent him to the prison. This lesson finds Joseph as a slave in the prison. Pharaoh sent some of his workers to prison, and Joseph's new assignment was to help them.

God did not reveal his purpose to Joseph. Despite Joseph's problems, he continued to show a high level of character and of leadership. God allowed Joseph to develop his character and his devotion to God while Joseph was a slave in the prison.

Even though the cupbearer forgot Joseph, God did not. Soon, Joseph will need every lesson that he learned in his life.

### WORDS OF OUR FAITH

• to be **faithful** -- to be loyal, dependable, and trustworthy

### ACTIVITY

You will need these items for this activity:

• 2 pitchers of water
• 2 cups
• 2 empty larger pitchers or larger buckets
• towels

Before class, place the pitchers of water at one end of the room. Place the empty pitchers or empty buckets at the opposite end. Place some towels by the empty pitchers.

Form two teams, and instruct them to form a line behind the pitchers of the water. Give the first person on each team a cup.

Say, **Today you will have the opportunity to be a cupbearer. Fill the cup with water from the pitcher. Take the cup to the other end of the room, and pour the water into your team's pitcher or bucket. If you spill any water, you must wait for a teammate to wipe up the water before you continue. Then hurry back to the line, and give the cup to the next person to fill. Continue the relay until your team's pitcher is empty, and all of the water is in your pitcher or bucket.**

After the game, say, **There is a cupbearer in our Bible study today. We will learn what happened to him.**

### BIBLICAL LESSON

Prepare a Bible story based on the lesson's scripture verses. Children will understand the lesson better if you tell them the story rather than reading it to them.

After the story, encourage the children to discuss the story by asking the following questions. This will help them apply it to their lives. There may not be a right or wrong answer.

1. **Have you ever had a dream that you did not understand?** Encourage the children to think about the dreams they experienced. Ask, **Is there one dream that you always remember? What do you think it meant? How did it affect you?**

2. **Have you ever done something nice for someone who forgot to repay the favor?**

3. **How does the memory verse, Proverbs 2:6, relate to this story?**

36

Say, **We had two exciting stories today! One story is about a cupbearer, and the other story is about a baker. Both men worked for the pharaoh of Egypt.**

Joseph lived a difficult life. He endured difficult situations in Egypt, but he stayed faithful to God. God worked through Joseph to interpret these two dreams.

God did not abandon Joseph. God will not abandon us when we face difficult times in our lives.

## MEMORY VERSE

Practice the study's memory verse. You will find suggestions for memory verse activities on pages 110.

## ADDITIONAL ACTIVITIES

Choose from these options to enhance the children's Bible study.

1.  Divide the children into two teams. Provide a space for children to draw. On small pieces of paper, write some words from the story, such as cup, vine, branches, grape, bread, bird, basket, and tree. Let one member from each team select a paper and draw the object for his or her team. Allow one minute for the team to guess the object.

2.  Create a skit to tell the story of Joseph, the cupbearer, the baker, and Pharaoh. Children may perform the skit for their families or for another class.

3.  Play a game or do an activity in the following section that relates to this lesson (p. 49ff).

# BASIC QUESTIONS

1.  Whom did Pharaoh put in the prison? (40:2-3)
    1. The chief cupbearer
    2. The chief baker
    **3. Both answers are correct.**

2.  Why were the faces of the cupbearer and the baker sad? (40:7-8)
    1. No one took care of them in the prison.
    **2. They had dreams, and no one could interpret them.**
    3. They were afraid of the guards.

3.  What did the men tell Joseph? (40:8, 16)
    **1. Their dreams**
    2. Their innocence
    3. Pharaoh's cruelty

4.  Who dreamed about the vine and the grapes? (40:9-10)
    1. Joseph
    2. The captain of the guard
    **3. The chief cupbearer**

5.  What would happen to the chief cupbearer? (40:13)
    **1. Pharaoh would restore him to his position.**
    2. Pharaoh would kill him.
    3. He would stay in the prison for two more years.

6.  Who dreamed about the baskets of bread? (40:16)
    1. The chief cupbearer
    **2. The chief baker**
    3. Pharaoh

7.  What would happen to the chief baker? (40:19)
    1. He would become the captain of the guard.
    **2. Pharaoh would kill him.**
    3. Pharaoh would restore him to his position.

8.  What happened three days after Joseph interpreted the dreams? (40:20)
    1. It was Pharaoh's birthday.
    2. Pharaoh gave a feast for all of his officials.
    **3. Both answers are correct.**

9.  Whom did Pharaoh restore? (40:21)
    **1. The chief cupbearer**
    2. The chief baker
    3. Joseph

10. What did the cupbearer forget? (40:23)
    1. He forgot to tell his wife and children about his dream.
    **2. He forgot to tell Pharaoh about Joseph.**
    3. He forgot to bow before the Pharaoh.

# LESSON 16

## Genesis 41:1-57
## Promoted!

**MEMORY VERSE:** "'I cannot do it,' Joseph replied to Pharaoh, 'but God will give Pharaoh the answer he desires.'" (Genesis 41:16)

**BIBLICAL TRUTH:** God honors those who are faithful to him.

### BIBLICAL COMMENTARY

In Study 8, God told Abraham that another nation would enslave his descendants for 400 years. However, God would rescue them. In this chapter, that begins to happen. Joseph was a major part of God's plan.

In this study, Joseph confronted a difficult challenge. He had the choice to take credit for the interpretation of the dreams, or to acknowledge that God was the one who provided the meaning of the dreams. Joseph decided to give credit to God. Joseph knew that Pharaoh controlled Joseph's life and his freedom. However, Joseph also trusted that God would be with him regardless of what happened.

In one sense, this is a story about how Joseph gains power and fame. But Joseph's story is part of a larger one about how God fulfilled the covenant with Abraham. Joseph was a direct descendant of Abraham, and he was a slave in Egypt. A famine approached. God needed a faithful man in a vital position. Joseph became the second person in command of Egypt. Only Pharaoh was higher in status.

This study will look at the early part of Joseph's story. Later, the students will learn about how God led Joseph's family to Egypt so that they could survive the upcoming famine.

### WORDS OF OUR FAITH

- to show **honor** -- to show respect to someone. We honor God when we say good things about him. We also honor God when we love and obey him.

### ACTIVITY

You will need this item for this activity:

- masking tape, or another way to create a boundary

Before class, use tape to mark a large square in the center of the room. The square should be large enough to accommodate all of the children. Another option is to take the children outside to play this game.

Say, **Pharaoh, the leader of Egypt, had two dreams. One of Pharaoh's dreams had cows in it. In this game, some players will pretend to be cows. The other players will try to catch the cows.**

Choose three children to catch the cows. These children must stay in the center area. The other children stand on one side of the room or outside the center area.

When you give the signal to start, the other children must cross the center section. The three children in the center will try to tag them. When a cowcatcher tags a cow, the child must remain inside the square. These cows are not allowed to help or hinder the cowcatchers.

The game is over when all of the cows are in the center or the time for this activity is finished.

### BIBLICAL LESSON

Prepare a Bible story based on the lesson's scripture verses. Children will understand the lesson better if you tell them the story rather than reading it to them.

After the story, encourage the children to discuss the story by asking the following questions. This will help them apply it to their lives. There may not be a right or wrong answer.

1. **God gave Pharaoh a message. Have you ever received a message from God? How did you react?**

2. **Joseph was in prison for two years before he heard about Pharaoh's dream. Have you ever**

waited a long time for God or someone else to fulfil a promise? How did you feel?

3. Joseph said that he could not interpret dreams. Instead, he said that God could do this. How do you give God credit for the things he does in your life?

Say, **God honored Joseph's faithfulness when he revealed to him the meaning of Pharaoh's dreams. Even though life was difficult for Joseph, God remembered him. Suddenly, Joseph's situation improved dramatically.**

**Have you ever experienced such a quick improvement in your life? God blessed Joseph because of his faithfulness. God honors us for our faithfulness to Him.**

## MEMORY VERSE

Practice the study's memory verse. You will find suggestions for memory verse activities on page.

## ADDITIONAL ACTIVITIES

Choose from these options to enhance the children's Bible study.

1. As a class, find three Bible verses that talk about God's care for his people.

2. Find a map of Egypt. As a class, research some facts about the nation of Egypt today.

3. Create a news story that tells about the appointment of Joseph as the second-in-command to Pharaoh. Write this story for presentation on television, radio, or the internet.

4. Play a game or do an activity in the following section that relates to this lesson (p. 49ff).

# BASIC QUESTIONS

1. *About what did Pharaoh dream? (41:2-7)*
   1. The cupbearer and Joseph
   **2. The cows and the corn**
   3. Both answers are correct.

2. *What did the ugly cows do in Pharaoh's dream? (41:4)*
   1. They stayed in the river.
   2. They ate the good corn.
   **3. They ate the fat cows.**

3. *What happened to the seven healthy heads of corn? (41:7)*
   **1. The seven thin heads of corn swallowed them.**
   2. The cows swallowed them.
   3. They became scorched.

4. *Whom did Pharaoh ask first to interpret his dreams? (41:8)*
   1. The chief cupbearer
   **2. The magicians and the wise men**
   3. Both answers are correct.

5. *Why did Pharaoh send for Joseph? (41:9-15)*
   1. The cupbearer told Pharaoh about Joseph.
   2. Pharaoh heard that Joseph interpreted some dreams.
   **3. Both answers are correct.**

6. *Who did Joseph say would give Pharaoh the answer he desired? (41:16)*
   **1. God**
   2. Joseph
   3. The magicians

7. *What would God do in Egypt? (41:29-32)*
   1. He would bring seven years of the abundance.
   2. He would bring seven years of the famine after the years of the abundance.
   **3. Both answers are correct.**

8. *What did Joseph say that Pharaoh should do? (41:33-35)*
   1. To begin to buy the grain from other countries
   **2. To collect the grain during the abundant years**
   3. To save the water in the wells

9. *Why did Pharaoh put Joseph in charge of the grain? (41:39-40)*
   1. God told Joseph everything about the famine.
   2. There was no one as discerning and wise as Joseph.
   **3. Both answers are correct.**

10. *Why did all of the countries come to Egypt to buy grain from Joseph? (41:57)*
    **1. The famine was severe in all of the world.**
    2. The grain in Egypt was the best in the world.
    3. Both answers are correct.

# LESSON 17

## Genesis 42:1-38
## Are you Spies?

**MEMORY VERSE:** "I am with you and will watch over you wherever you go, and I will bring you back to this land. I will not leave you until I have done what I have promised you." (Genesis 28:15)

**BIBLICAL TRUTH:** We honor God when we obey him.

### BIBLICAL COMMENTARY

The covenant God established with Abraham in Genesis 15 was threatened many times throughout history. In this story, the famine had the potential to kill Jacob and his family and halt the lineage of Abraham. However, God fulfilled his promise. Jacob's heirs remained alive. Also, Jacob's family went to Egypt to buy food along with other Canaanites.

Joseph controlled the lives of his brothers. They bowed before Joseph as his dreams predicted. Joseph had a choice to make. Would he get revenge on his brothers, or would he show grace to them in their time of need?

Verse 24 gives a glimpse into Joseph's thoughts. Joseph wept as his brothers recalled their sin against him. Yet, Joseph was unsure of their motives. Joseph had a plan to test the strength and honesty of these men. How would they respond? Did they learn their lesson?

Study 18 will continue to reveal God's plan and Joseph's obedience in one of the most memorable family dramas in the Bible.

### ACTIVITY

The teacher will play the role of Joseph. Stand and face the students. Say, **I am Joseph. I will give you instructions to do various actions, and I want you to imitate my actions. Listen for these words: "Joseph says." Imitate only the actions that follow the words "Joseph says." If I say, "Joseph says, 'Raise your hand,'"** then imitate my action. **If I say, "Raise your hand," do not imitate my action because I did not say, "Joseph says."**

Practice a few times to make sure that the children understand how to play the game. Use various commands and demonstrate the actions. Sometimes, begin with "Joseph says."

These commands can include the following actions: pat your head, smile, wave hello, flex your muscles, touch your toes, turn around, and sit down. You may add your own commands to make the game longer.

Say, **In this activity you listened to the command. Then you decided whether to imitate my action. When I said, "Joseph says," you imitated my action because I was in charge. I had power.**

**Today we will learn that Joseph had power over Egypt. We will learn what he did with that power.**

### BIBLICAL LESSON

Prepare a Bible story based on the lesson's scripture verses. Children will understand the lesson better if you tell them the story rather than reading it to them.

After the story, encourage the children to discuss the story by asking the following questions. This will help them apply it to their lives. There may not be a right or wrong answer.

1. **Has anyone wronged you and later needed your help? What did you do?**

2. **When the brothers found the silver in the sack, they asked, "What is this that God has done to us?" Did God really do that to them? Have you ever blamed God for your troubles?**

3. **Why do you think Joseph's brothers did not recognize him?**

40

Say, **Joseph experienced a difficult life. His brothers hated him, and they sold him to merchants who took him to a foreign land. He worked as a household slave, and he unjustly became a prisoner. Through all of this, God was with Joseph. God worked to save Joseph's family and to bring healing and peace to Joseph's brothers.**

**Joseph was now in a place of authority. How would Joseph respond when his brothers learned who he was?**

**Everyone makes choices. We can bring honor to God by making right choices. Joseph brought honor to God by his choices and his attitude.**

## MEMORY VERSE

Practice the study's memory verse. You will find suggestions on page 110.

## ADDITIONAL ACTIVITIES

Choose from these options to enhance the children's Bible study.

1. As a group, find answers to these questions: What is a famine? What causes a famine? What effect does a famine have on the economy and on the people? Is there a famine anywhere in the world now? How can you help people who experience famine? Help children prepare a report on their research.

2. Ask, **Why did Joseph's brothers not recognize him? How did Joseph recognize his brothers? How did their actions fulfil Joseph's dreams?** Have children act out this story with dialogue that answers these questions.

3. Play a game or do an activity in the following section that relates to this lesson (p. 49ff).

# BASIC QUESTIONS

1. *Which brother did not go to Egypt? (42:4)*
   1. Simeon
   2. **Benjamin**
   3. Reuben

2. *Why did Jacob not want to send Benjamin to Egypt? (42:4)*
   1. **Harm might come to Benjamin.**
   2. Benjamin was sick.
   3. Benjamin watched the flocks.

3. *In front of whom did the brothers bow down? (42:6)*
   1. The governor
   2. Joseph
   3. **Both answers are correct.**

4. *Who was recognized when the brothers asked Joseph for food? (42:8)*
   1. Joseph and his brothers recognized each other.
   2. **Joseph recognized his brothers, but they did not recognize him.**
   3. Joseph did not recognize his brothers.

5. *What did Joseph say his brothers were? (42:14)*
   1. **Spies**
   2. Shepherds
   3. His brothers

6. *Why did Joseph keep one of his brothers in the prison while the other brothers returned to their home? (42:16-20)*
   1. They told Joseph that they were spies.
   2. **Joseph wanted to learn if they told the truth.**
   3. They did not pay for their grain.

7. *When did Joseph weep? (42:21-24)*
   1. **His brothers said they received punishment for what they did to Joseph.**
   2. He received bad news from Pharaoh.
   3. Both answers are correct.

8. *What did the brothers find in their sacks of grain? (42:27)*
   1. **Their silver**
   2. Stolen jewels from the home of Joseph
   3. Both answers are correct.

9. *What did Jacob say when Joseph's brothers told him what happened? (42:36)*
   1. **"Everything is against me."**
   2. "If I must send Benjamin, I will."
   3. "Why did the governor put you in prison?"

10. *Who promised to bring back Benjamin? (42:37)*
    1. Simeon
    2. **Reuben**
    3. Jacob

# LESSON 18

## Genesis 43:1-15, 23b-32; 44:1-18, 33-34
## Face To Face

**MEMORY VERSE:** "Be kind and compassionate to one another, forgiving each other, just as in Christ God forgave you." (Ephesians 4:32)

**BIBLICAL TRUTH:** God forgives us, and he wants us to forgive others.

### BIBLICAL COMMENTARY

Israel instructed his sons to return to Egypt and to buy more food. This seemed simple, but Judah reminded his father that Joseph commanded them to return with Benjamin.

Israel was old and desperate. He spoke of trouble, bereavement, mistakes, and mercy. When Israel had no other choices left, he agreed to send his sons back to Egypt. He said that he would die of sorrow if Benjamin did not return safely. As the brothers watched their father's lament, they felt guilty. The brothers were responsible for the loss of Joseph. Could they guarantee the safe return of Benjamin?

In Egypt, Joseph was kind toward his family, but he was resolute in his plan. Joseph did not plan revenge on his brothers, but he tested their attitudes. Joseph wondered if his brothers treated Benjamin as they treated him. Were the brothers truly repentant?

Judah promised his life for Benjamin's safety. Judah asked that Joseph take him as a slave instead of Benjamin. In the crisis, the brothers revealed their attitudes.

### WORDS OF OUR FAITH

- **mercy** -- forgiveness or kindness to those who did what was wrong.
- **compassion** -- concern for others that leads us to help them.
- the **steward** -- a trusted member of Joseph's household. He was in charge of Joseph's house and business affairs.

- **bereavement** -- a sad feeling because someone very close has died.
- **divination** -- a way to discover knowledge through the study of objects, signs, or supernatural powers.

### ACTIVITY

You will need these items for this activity:

- a cup
- a piece of wood
- two boxes

Before class, place the piece of wood in one box. Place the cup in the other box. Close the boxes. You can cover them with a cloth or close the top of the box. Make sure that a child cannot see what is inside the boxes.

Divide the class into teams. Say, **Today we will try to find a cup. One of these boxes has a cup inside. The other box has a piece of wood. Each team will take a turn as it sends a member to choose one of the boxes. If a player chooses the box with the block of wood, the player returns to the team. If the player chooses the box with the cup, the player must go to the other team and become a member of that team.**

Let each child take a turn, as time permits. After every turn, replace the items in each box. Do not let the children see.

At the end of the game, count the team members. The team with the most members is the winner.

Say, **The brothers of Joseph found a silver cup in Benjamin's bag. Joseph said that the person who owned that bag would become his slave.**

### BIBLICAL LESSON

Prepare a Bible story based on the lesson's scripture verses. Children will understand the lesson better if you tell them the story rather than reading it to them.

After the story, encourage the children to discuss the story by asking the following questions. This will help them apply it to their lives. There may not be a right or wrong answer.

1. Judah promised to protect Benjamin. Have you ever had a friend, a brother, or a sister whom you protected? How did you feel about that person?

2. Joseph did not reveal his identity to his brothers. Why not? How do you treat people who have done wrong things to you?

3. Joseph was emotionally moved by the sight of his brother, Benjamin. Have you ever seen something that made you cry? Did you ever cry when you saw someone? Talk about this experience.

4. Have you ever watched someone suffer? Did that person hurt you in the past? Were you tempted to hurt the person, even though he or she needed help?

Say, **Joseph had this choice. His brothers sold him into slavery, and they lied to his father. Now they were at his mercy. He recognized them, but they did not recognize him. Joseph had the authority to condemn his brothers to death. However, he chose not to take revenge on them.**

**God forgives us, and he wants us to forgive others. God will help us forgive others and resolve our conflicts.**

## MEMORY VERSE

Practice the study's memory verse. You will find suggestions on page 110.

## ADDITIONAL ACTIVITIES

Choose from these options to enhance the children's Bible study.

1. Have the children dramatize the search through the sacks. You can use the items from the activity earlier in this lesson.

2. Judah offered to replace Benjamin as Joseph's slave. He asked to take the place of Benjamin. How is this similar to the way Jesus became a sacrifice for our sins?

3. Research the distance between Egypt and Israel. How far did Joseph's brothers need to travel? Draw their route on a map.

4. Play a game or do an activity in the following section that relates to this lesson (p. 49ff).

# BASIC QUESTIONS

*1. Why did Israel send his sons back to Egypt?.(43:1-2)*
    1. The famine was still severe.
    2. They ate all of the grain that they had.
    **3. Both answers are correct.**

*2. Who said he would bring Benjamin back safely? (43:8-9)*
    1. Israel
    **2. Judah**
    3. Simeon

*3. What did the brothers bring to give to Joseph? (43:11-13)*
    1. The silver that was put in their sacks
    2. The gifts they brought
    **3. Both answers are correct.**

*4. Who took the brothers to Joseph's house? (43:24)*
    **1. Joseph's steward**
    2. The captain of the guard
    3. Joseph

*5. About whom did Joseph ask the brothers? (43:26-27)*
    1. Simeon
    2. Reuben
    **3. Their father**

*6. Which brother caused Joseph to be moved deeply? (43:29-30)*
    **1. Benjamin**
    2. Simeon
    3. Judah

*7. What did the steward put in Benjamin's sack? (44:1-2)*
    1. Silver
    2. Joseph's silver cup
    **3. Both answers are correct.**

*8. What happened after the brothers left Egypt? (44:4)*
    1. Traders sold them more grain.
    **2. Joseph sent his steward after them.**
    3. Thieves stole their grain.

*9. Why did the brothers throw themselves at Joseph's feet? (44:14-16)*
    1. They thought all of them would die.
    **2. They thought all of them would become slaves.**
    3. Both answers are correct.

*10. What did Judah say to Joseph? (44:33)*
    1. Let me become your slave instead of the boy.
    2. Let the boy return with his brothers.
    **3. Both answers are correct.**

# LESSON 19

## Genesis 45:1-46:7
## I Am Joseph

**MEMORY VERSE:** "But God sent me ahead of you to preserve for you a remnant on earth and to save your lives by a great deliverance." (Genesis 45:7)

**BIBLICAL TRUTH:** God works through the people who obey him.

### BIBLICAL COMMENTARY

Joseph knew that his brothers had changed their attitudes! Emotions overcame him as he made his revelation to his brothers, "I am Joseph!" Joseph acknowledged the sin of his brothers, but he did not condemn them or punish them. Joseph acknowledged that God worked through the entire series of events. He said, "Do not be angry with yourselves for selling me here, because it was to save lives that God sent me ahead of you." He truly forgave his brothers, and he affirmed God's care for him.

Pharaoh told Joseph to bring his entire family to Egypt, where Pharaoh would give them the best of the land. The brothers returned to their father with the good news that Joseph was alive. There was anticipation of a grand and glorious reunion between Joseph and his father. Jacob eagerly planned to leave Canaan and to go to Egypt.

### WORDS OF OUR FAITH

- a **remnant** -- a small group that survives an event that destroyed the majority of the people.

### ACTIVITY

You will need this item for this activity:

- a blindfold

Say, **Sometimes we recognize people by their voices. Can you tell who someone is when you hear his or her voice? Our game today will give you the opportunity to do that.**

Place a blindfold on one child. Choose another child to call out, "Here I am. Who am I?" The caller may try to disguise his or her voice. The blindfolded child must guess the name of the caller. If the blindfolded child does not guess the first time, have the caller give a hint. As time permits, allow every child who wants to play to have a turn.

Ask, **What made it difficult to recognize a voice?** (The voice was not clear, it sounded different, or the blindfolded child could not remember the caller's name.) **When we do not see people for a long time, they change so much that we do not recognize them. Sometimes we do not recognize people when we see them in an unexpected place. Have you ever experienced these things?** (Let the children respond.)

**When Joseph's brothers arrived in Egypt, did they recognize him? Did they expect to find him there? Our lesson to- day continues the story of Joseph and his brothers.**

### BIBLICAL LESSON

Prepare a Bible story based on the lesson's scripture verses. Children will understand the lesson better if you tell them the story rather than reading it to them.

After the story, encourage the children to discuss the story by asking the following questions. This will help them apply it to their lives. There may not be a right or wrong answer.

1. **What is the biggest surprise that you experienced?**

2. **Why do you think the brothers were scared when they realized who Joseph was? How would you feel?**

3. **Joseph had mercy on his brothers. Has anyone been merciful to you? Do you think you deserved mercy?**

Say, **God worked to bring this family together. Joseph had a godly attitude, because he loved and obeyed God. The brothers received mercy even though they deserved punishment. God worked in the lives of Joseph's family, and he still works in our lives today.**

## MEMORY VERSE
Practice the study's memory verse. You will find suggestions on page 110.

## ADDITIONAL ACTIVITIES
1. Choose from these options to enhance the children's Bible study.

2. Create a family tree for Joseph. Include his wife, children, brothers, parents, and grandparents.

3. Have each child create a family tree for his or her family. Have the children research the names of their grandparents and great-grandparents as far back as they are able.

4. Make a timeline of everything that happened to Joseph. Start when his father gave him the coat of many colors and end with his father's move to Egypt.

5. Play a game or do an activity in the following section that relates to this lesson (p. 49ff).

# BASIC QUESTIONS

1. *What did Joseph do when he could no longer control himself? (45:1-3)*
   1. He gave the donkeys to his brothers.
   **2. He told his brothers who he was.**
   3. He returned all of the brothers' silver.

2. *About whom did Joseph ask his brothers? (45:3)*
   **1. His father**
   2. His mother
   3. The children of his brothers

3. *Who did Joseph say sent him to Egypt? (45:5)*
   1. His brothers
   2. Jacob
   **3. God**

4. *Why did God send Joseph ahead of his brothers? (45:7)*
   1. To preserve a remnant, a small group that survives
   2. To save lives
   **3. Both answers are correct.**

5. *What were the brothers to tell Jacob? (45:9)*
   1. Joseph is the lord of all of Egypt.
   2. Come down to me; don't delay.
   **3. Both answers are correct.**

6. *Who told Joseph to bring his father to Egypt? (45:17-18)*
   1. The priests and magicians
   **2. Pharaoh**
   3. His brothers

7. *How did Jacob respond when the brothers told him that Joseph was alive? (27:25)*
   **1. He was stunned, and he did not believe them.**
   2. He believed them right away.
   3. Both answers are correct.

8. *What did Israel decide to do after he knew that Joseph was alive? (45:28)*
   1. To order Joseph to come to him
   **2. To go to Egypt and to see Joseph**
   3. To stay where he was

9. *What happened at Beersheba? (46:1-4)*
   1. Israel offered sacrifices.
   2. God told Israel not to be afraid to go to Egypt.
   **3. Both answers are correct.**

10. *Who promised to bring Jacob back from Egypt? (46:4)*
    **1. God**
    2. Joseph
    3. Both answers are correct.

# LESSON 20

## Genesis 46:28-32; 50:14-26
## Promises Fulfilled

**MEMORY VERSE:** "But God will surely come to your aid and take you up out of this land to the land he promised on oath to Abraham, Isaac and Jacob." (Genesis 50:24b)

**BIBLICAL TRUTH**: God loves people, and keeps his promises.

### BIBLICAL COMMENTARY

This study brings both resolution and unanswered questions for the family of Israel. The family was safe in Egypt from famine. However, Joseph reminded them that they would not remain in Egypt forever. The family must return to Canaan to fulfil God's promise in Genesis 15. Canaan was the land that God promised Abraham, Isaac, and Jacob.

Joseph and Jacob were reunited. However, the brothers were afraid of Joseph. Approximately 17 years passed between Jacob's arrival in Egypt and his death. During this time, the brothers lived comfortably under the protection of Joseph. However, they worried that he protected them only because Jacob was alive. Joseph forgave the brothers a long time before Jacob died. Because of this, he wept when his brothers spoke about their fear.

Did the brothers ever rid themselves of the guilt they carried? The Bible does not say. However, the lives of Joseph, Jacob, and the brothers showed the effects of true forgiveness and reconciliation. Jacob's sons demonstrated how a lack of forgiveness can bring spiritual bondage. At the end of this study, both Jacob and Joseph died.

### WORDS OF OUR FAITH

to **glorify** -- to give honor or praise to someone or something.

### ACTIVTY

You will need these items for this activity:
• a piece of yarn or tape

Before class, use tape or yarn to mark a path to another place in your building or area. For best results, mark a path that has several turns. Meet with your class at the beginning of the path.

Say, **Jacob needed directions to Goshen. He sent Judah to ask Joseph for directions. Today you will give me directions to a location in our area. On the ground, there is a path that is visible. You will give me directions that follow the path. Be specific!**

As the children give you directions, interpret the directions as literally as possible. Only stop when the children tell you to stop. Do not turn unless you are instructed to turn. If you are instructed to turn, rotate slowly until the children tell you to stop. Continue to follow the directions until you arrive at the destination.

Say, **Jacob followed the directions that Joseph gave to Judah. At the end of his travels, Jacob met Joseph.**

**When we receive directions from God, we must follow them. God guides us to good things.**

### BIBLICAL LESSON

Prepare a Bible story based on the lesson's scripture verses. Children will understand the lesson better if you tell them the story rather than reading it to them.

After the story, encourage the children to discuss the story by asking the following questions. This will help them apply it to their lives. There may not be a right or wrong answer.

1. **Joseph forgave his brothers for what they did. He did this even though the brothers did something wrong to him. Have you ever forgiven someone who did something extremely wrong against you? Was it easy or difficult? Why?**

2. **Joseph's brothers were afraid that Joseph would punish them for what they did. Have you ever felt guilty for something that you did to someone else? How did your guilt affect your relationship to that person?**

Say, **During his years in Egypt, Joseph did not know what would happen to him. However, he remained faithful to God. Joseph was very happy when he was reunited with his father.**

**Like Joseph, we do not know what will happen in our lives. However, God wants us to be faithful to him. God is the main character of Genesis because he saved and healed Jacob's family. God worked through Jacob and his sons to bring the family back together again.**

## MEMORY VERSE

Practice the study's memory verse. You will find suggestions on page 110.

## ADDITIONAL ACTIVITIES

Choose from these options to enhance the children's Bible study.

1. Pretend to be Joseph and his brothers. As a class, write a letter of apology from Joseph's brothers to Joseph. Then, write a letter of forgiveness from Joseph to his brothers.

2. With the information you learned, create a family tree of Abraham's family. List the descendants of Abraham, Isaac, Jacob, and Joseph.

3. Write a song about Joseph and his brothers. Use a familiar melody for the music. Write the lyrics as a class.

4. Play a game or do an activity in the following section that relates to this lesson (p. 49ff).

# BASIC QUESTIONS

*1. How did Jacob get to Goshen? (46:28)*
   1. Pharaoh sent someone to show the way.
   2. Joseph travelled with them.
   **3. Jacob sent Judah to get the directions.**

*2. When did Joseph go to Goshen? (46:29)*
   1. A week after Jacob arrived
   **2. When Jacob arrived in Goshen**
   3. Joseph never went to Goshen.

*3. What happened when Joseph finally appeared before Israel? (46:29)*
   1. Joseph threw his arms around his father.
   2. Joseph wept for a long time.
   **3. Both answers are correct.**

*4. After Jacob died, why did the brothers worry? (50:15)*
   **1. They thought that Joseph would pay them back for all the wrongs that they did to him.**
   2. They thought that Pharaoh would not show kindness to them anymore.
   3. Both answers are correct.

*5. What did Joseph say when the brothers threw themselves before him? (50:18-19)*
   1. "Don't be afraid."
   2. "Am I in the place of God?"
   **3. Both answers are correct.**

*6. What did Joseph say he would do? (50:21)*
   1. He would force his brothers to leave Goshen.
   **2. He would provide for his brothers and for their children.**
   3. He would make slaves of his brothers.

*7. Who had intended everything that happened to Joseph for good? (50:20)*
   1. Jacob
   **2. God**
   3. Pharaoh

*8. Where would God take Jacob's family? (50:24)*
   1. God told them to stay in Egypt forever.
   **2. God would lead them to the land that he promised to them.**
   3. Both answers are correct.

*9. What did Joseph tell the sons of Israel to do when they left Egypt? (50:25)*
   1. To write everything that happened to them
   **2. To carry his bones from Egypt to the Promised Land**
   3. Both answers are correct.

*10. What happened to Joseph? (50:22-23, 26)*
   1. He lived to see three generations of Ephraim's children.
   2. He died at 110 years old.
   **3. Both answers are correct.**

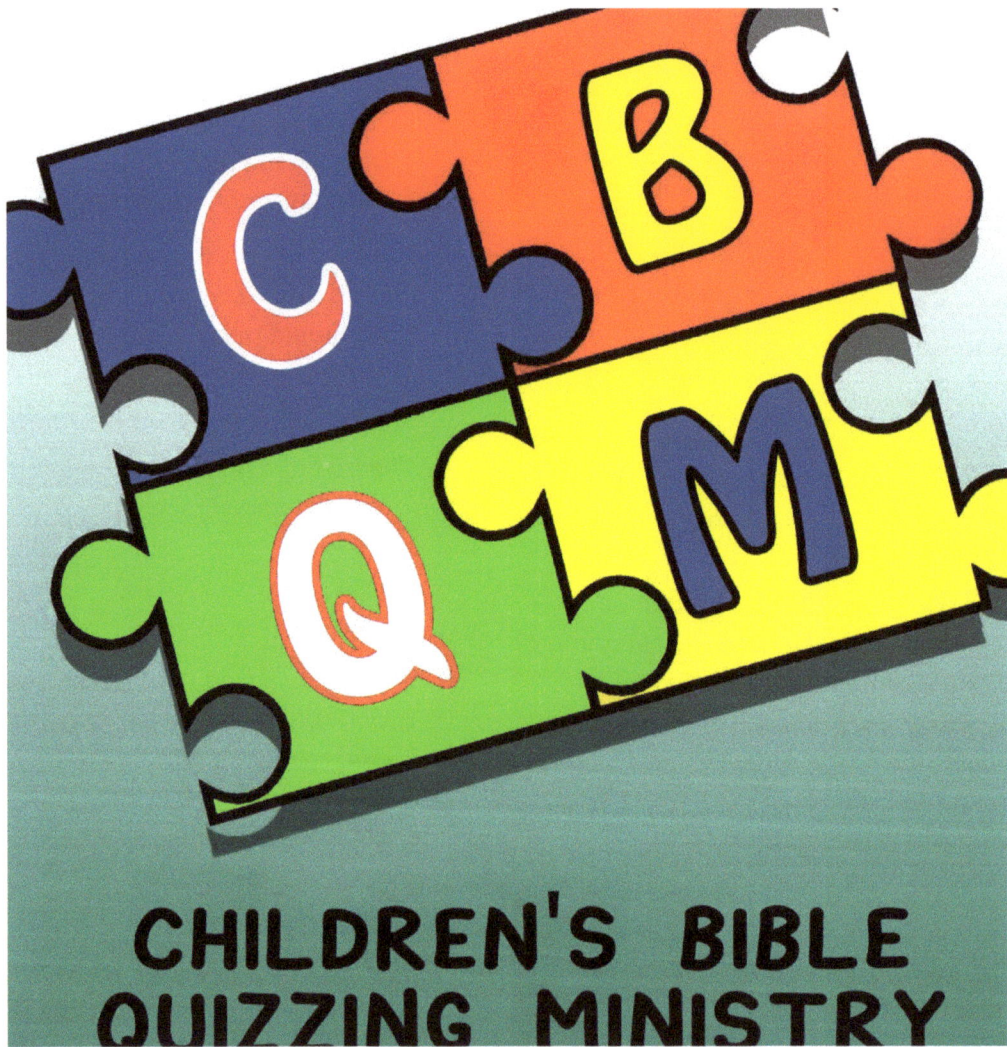

CHILDREN'S BIBLE
QUIZZING MINISTRY

# What is Children's Bible Quizzing Ministry (CBQM) Activity based quizzing?

The Church of the Nazarene has always set aside a special space for children. Jesus Christ himself did it when he strongly told his disciples not to separate the children because theirs is the kingdom of heaven. "Starting children off on the way they should go" (Proverbs 22: 6) is a pressing mandate that the Lord gives us, especially in our convoluted societies in which our children are dying physically and spiritually. Children's Bible Quizzing Ministry - Activities, known by its acronym as CBQM, was derived from the need to deepen and energize the Bible study for children. It is considered a powerful and effective tool for evangelism and children's discipleship in local churches .

Starting from the playful principle (learning by playing), CBQM - Activities consists of a series of games divided into the categories of memorization, reflection, arts and crafts, acting and music. (This is different than the traditional style of Children's Bible Quizzing using questions and answers.) Each of the games is related to, or has been adapted to, the subject of study. Each local church forms a team with 10 members between 7 and 11 years old. (They can be under 7 years old, but it is recommended that they be children who already know how to read and write.) This team will be prepared by a coach throughout the year. The head of the district Children's Ministries plans a demonstration (competition) in which each team demonstrates what they have learned from the Bible through the games that they participate in. The team that demonstrates greater preparation, by accumulating points, will represent their district in a national demonstration. However, it should be clear that the goal is to learn the Word of God, not to compete.

We trust that this attractive and experiential teaching will allow children to treasure the Word of God in their hearts and that "they will not depart from the right path" even if they leave childhood behind.

## Mission:
To prepare children as disciples of Jesus by studying and treasuring God's Word in their hearts.

## Vision:
To be an effective means of evangelism and a dynamic tool of discipleship.

## Values:
We are moved by Christian values such as love, fellowship, and commitment. This ministry also promotes teamwork, collaboration, respect, among many others among children.

## What Resources Do I Need?

✓ NIV Bible

✓ CBQM Manual (You can visit the Discipleship Ministries page for this and other resources: www.SdmiResources.MesoamericaRegion.org

✓ Teaching materials (paper, paint, glue, scissors, pens, crayons, colored paper, etc.)

## How do I form a team in my local church?

The **local SDMI President** must get the materials that are available for CBQM (physical copy or download electronic copies), and select a brother / sister who is helpful, dynamic and who loves working with children to work as a team coach.

**Coach** - his/her function is to prepare the team, motivating them to study the Word, giving or coordinating the Bible lessons, leading the learning activities and games, accompanying the team to all the quiz demonstrations organized by the district, etc.

**Team** – the team will consist of a maximum of 10 children from 7 to 11 years of age. (They may be younger, but they should be able to read and write.) If a child reaches 12 years between the months of July-December, they can still participate.

## How Do We Prepare The Children?

A teaching and study time must be established with the team. The study must consider the theme assigned for the bible quizzing.

To study the subject better, it can be divided into chapters or specific events, for this use the coach's guide which will guide you in this process. Start with teaching about the events, and discuss with them by using questions and having them answer from memory about situations, characters, places and names. Explain facts that motivate the curiosity of the team in terms of customs, meaning of objects or rites and other interesting features that complement and clarify the text and context read. Create lists of words, names, places, objects, animals. Find out in which other books of the Bible the main characters are mentioned. Have the children memorize the key verses exactly. Help the children memorize events and sequences of the stories, in a non-textual way, so they can relate it as completely as possible. It is necessary to help them remember important data. Guide them to discover individually and as a team the teaching of God for their lives and perform the games that are related to the lesson studied.

**THIS STUDY GUIDE CAN HELP WITH THE FOLLOWING THEMES:**

- Where did this character(s) come from?
- Who are they related to?
- Where does the story unfold?
- How does God work in their lives?
- What is the reason why this story is found in the Bible?
- How does this passage relate to Christ and therefore to salvation?
- Take each story and bring it to the current time. How would you do it?
- What values are found in the story?
- What places are mentioned? Find them on a map.
- What are the characters like?
- What characteristics do they have?
- What things stand out in the culture and do you need to investigate (animals, crafts, rites or customs)?

**IN ADDITION:**

- Invite Sunday School teachers and / or people with theological studies to teach lessons about the topic and answer questions.
- Encourage people of the church to support the team.
- Practice each game only after having studied and clarified the subject considerably.
- Remember that it is important to establish the skills in which the child performs best.

# Who are the officials in a Demonstration?

**Moderator** – He or she must be an impartial person. They can be a guest from another district or from a local church that is not participating in the demonstration.
- This is the person who chooses the games and prepares the material for them.
- Directs the competition.
- Reads the instructions for each category or game.
- Chooses the team of judges.

**Judges** - They must be impartial. They can be invited from another district or from a church that is not participating.

A judge will be assigned to each participating team. That is, if there are 5 teams participating, there must be 5 judges. They must:
- Ensure that the rules of each game are kept.
- Oversee the participant(s) from that team during each game.
- Let the moderator know if any rules are broken.

**Time Judge** – They must keep time for each game, giving the signal for the start and the end of the time allotted for the game.

## ANNUAL STUDY CYCLE
- GENESIS: 2019-2020
- EXODUS: 2020-2021
- JOSHUA, JUDGES & RUTH: 2021-2022
- 1 & 2 SAMUEL: 2022–2023
- MATTHEW: 2023-2024
- ACTS: 2024-2025

## NOTES

If you have worked with CBQM - Activities before, you will notice some changes. For example, we have changed the word "trainer" to "coach" because we think it is more appropriate.

Some games have been modified, others have been removed and new games directly related to the subject of study have been added.

Remember that a competition is a demonstration, because each team demonstrates how much they have learned from the Word of God. We must ensure that competitiveness is healthy and creates bonds of friendship between the participating teams.

# Letter to the Coach (Testimony)

Hello beloved brother or sister,

My name is Pamela Vargas, I want to greet you with the affection that characterizes us as Christians. In 2007, my mother was the president of SDMI in our local church. She didn't know anything about CBQM-Activities, and I didn't know much more than that. She asked me if I wanted to be in charge of it and I accepted. What I never imagined was that I would find in this ministry a call so powerful that I am still passionate about it after all this time. I can even say that it is through this ministry that I have been able to study the Word of God in a responsible and constant way.

Our church had already participated in CBQM-Activities once before, so I talked to Jaqueline to see if she would like to help me since she had some experience from the previous time. I remember that year the study book was Acts. We were so excited as we started looking for the children who would form the team: Diana, Marcela, Adrián, Emily, Steve, Ester and Ruth (all of them became dear to my heart). We had designated Saturday afternoons as our time to study and practice. Our team was called "Missionaries of Christ." We noticed that the ministry needed consistency, perseverance and continuous motivation of the children. At times it was difficult, but we were convinced of something ... they needed to learn the bible. When we began to see the first fruits, the joint efforts of parents and the interest of the team, everything was worth it.

Sister Cristy, mother of Diana, Marcela and Adrián, told me with joy that Diana said that when she grew up she would be the coach of the team. Today I belong to a church where Verónica is the pastor and mother of Emily and Steve, and it is precisely they who are coaching the CBQM team. I have only given them support when they needed it.

I have thought and rethought about the responsibility that I accepted back in 2007 without knowing what exactly I was getting myself into. I understand now that our purpose for God's kingdom is always before us to accept and pursue.

I am sure that once you start with this ministry, you will be as passionate about it as I am. It is my prayer that God will provide you with strength, wisdom, and resources, but above all, the love to sow the powerful seed of the gospel in the fertile hearts of children through this fun way. Never give up; you'll see it's worth it all.

In Christ

Pamela Vargas
pdepamela@gmail.com

# Team Name

## Instructions:

1. In advance and with the help of the coach, each team must choose a name.
2. The name must be related to the subject of study.
3. It must have biblical support which will be explained by one or more participants.
4. At this time, the team members must also be presented.
5. Judges should consider the following aspects:
   - The relationship to the subject of study
   - Creativity of the name
   - Biblical reference
   - Creativity of presentation
   - Mention of the team members

## Foul:

Points are deducted from a team if anyone is talking while another team is presenting.

**Points**

100 points

**Time**

Less than 5 minutes

**Participants**

The whole team

**Mode**

One team at a time

# Distinctive

## Instructions:

1. In advance and with the help of the coach and parents, each team must carry/wear something that distinguishes them. It can be a shirt, cap, sports uniform, etc. It can include the name of the team, the member's name and a logo.
2. The judges evaluate according to the following scale:
   - Uniformity (all the same)
   - Badge Creativity
   - Presentation creativity

## Foul:

Points are deducted from a team if anyone is talking while another team is presenting.

**Points**

50 points

**Time**

Less than 5 minutes

**Participants**

The whole team

**Mode**

One team at a time

# Team Cheer

## Instructions:

1. In advance and with the help of the coach, each team must prepare a team cheer.
2. It should be based on the subject of study and the name of the team.
3. It may not contain offensive ideas or words towards other teams.
4. The judges evaluate according to the following scale:
   - Relevance to the subject of study
   - Cheer creativity
   - Creativity in Presentation
   - Mention of team name

## Foul:

Points are deducted from a team if anyone is talking while another team is presenting.

**Points**

50 points

**Time**

Less than 5 minutes

**Participants**

The whole team

**Mode**

One team at a time

# Mascot

## Instructions:

1. In advance and with the help of the coach, each team must have a mascot.
2. Preferably it should be an animal that is related to the subject of study.
3. It must contain a biblical teaching.
4. The judges evaluate according to the following scale:
   - Relevance to the subject of study
   - Costume Creativity
   - Creativity of Presentation
   - Biblical teaching

## Foul:

Points are deducted from a team if anyone is talking while another team is presenting.

**Points**

100 points

**Time**

Less than 5 minutes

**Participants**

The whole team

**Mode**

One team at a time

# Team banner

## Instructions:

1. In advance and with the help of the coach, each team must have a team banner.
2. It must be related to the name of the team.
3. It must be drawn and painted by the team participants and will serve to decorate their space at a demonstration.
4. It must be related to the subject of study and biblical support which will be explained by one or more participants.
5. The judges evaluate according to the following scale:
   - Relevance to the subject of study
   - Drawing creativity
   - Order and cleanliness
   - Biblical teaching
   - Creativity in the presentation

## Foul:

Points are deducted from a team if anyone is talking while another team is presenting.

## Points

100 points

## Time

Less than 5 minutes

## Participants

The whole team

## Mode

One team at a time

# MEMORIZATION CATEGORY

Memorization and reasoning are fundamental for learning, and repetition is one of the keys to memorization. The objective of this category is to help children memorize and understand the Bible in a dynamic and attractive way.

SOME MEMORIZATION TECHNIQUES:
- Connect and link
- Associate objects with places
- Create stories
- Link words with numbers to remember sequences
- Draw mental maps
- Acronyms, using the first letter of each word
- Repeat the keywords
- Use all the senses

For a local, district, zone, national demonstration, etc. the moderator will choose:

# 3 Memorization Games

The teams will know which specific games will be played ONLY on the day of the demonstration.

# Advance

## Instructions:

1. The moderator draws the order in which the teams participate and they are placed in front of their three rings (hula hoops).

2. The first participant must say a verse from the list of memory verses (their choice). They must say it exactly; if it is correct, the moderator indicates it and the participant advances into the first ring.

3. The next participant must recite another verse (their choice); the difficulty is that they cannot recite a verse that has already been quoted by another participant; in case this happens, the child will not be able to advance.

If during the first 30 seconds the child does not begin to say his verse, he loses the opportunity and does not advance.

10 points are awarded for each verse correctly quoted, up to 30 points per team

## Consultations:
Are not permitted.

## Foul:
If someone from the audience says a part of the passage or reference out loud, or if the child consults with their coach or team, their participation in this game is disqualified and canceled.

## Suggestion:
If there are many teams participating, it can be reduced to 2 rings per team.

## Example:

### Points
10 points for correct passage

### Time
30 seconds to start

### Participants
1 per team

### Mode
One team at a time alternating

### Materials
- Three hoops (hula hoops) per team.
- The judge must have the list of the memory passages.

Isabel of team "Genesis" quoted two passages, advancing 2 rings, earning 20 points.

James of team "Noah" quoted 3 passages, advancing 3 rings, earning 30 points.

Cammy from team "In the Beginning" quoted 1 passage, advancing 1 ring, earning 10 points for her team.

# Stop

## Instructions:

1. The moderator will give 1 answer sheet to each team with the following titles: LETTER; NAME OF PERSON; OBJECT, ANIMAL or PLANT; PLACE; and TOTAL. (See example below.)
2. The moderator starts the game by beginning to recite the alphabet in a loud voice, starting with the letter "A" and continues the alphabet in a low voice. A judge will say STOP! at a certain point, and the game with start with the letter that the moderator was saying when the judge said STOP! The moderator will say the first letter to be used for the game, and then begins the count of 2 minutes for the participants to answer.
3. The child who finishes his/her answer sheet first must say out loud, "STOP!" Then the other participants will no longer be able to fill in more answers.
4. Next, a second letter will be chosen, and the 2nd round begins. After playing the two suggested rounds, the children hand in their answer sheets. If there are correct words that are repeated on the answer sheets of other participants, those answers receive 5 points each. For the answers that are correct and not repeated, they receive 10 points each.

## Consultations:

Are not permitted.

## Foul:

If the judge sees that a participant continues to fill out their sheet after another participant has said, STOP! All boxes are cleared.

## Suggestion:

If there were many teams participating, you can use two letters. If fewer, you can use 3 letters.

## Points

The accumulated amount on the answer sheet

## Time

2 minutes

## Participants

1 per team

## Mode

Simultaneous

## Materials

- One answer sheet per team
- One pen per team

| NAME: Lucas Álvarez | | | | | TEAM: Genesis | | |
|---|---|---|---|---|---|---|---|
| LETRA | NAME OF PERSON | points | OBJECT, ANIMAL OR PLANT | points | PLACE | points | TOTAL |
| E | Eve | 10 | Almonds | 10 | Egypt | 5 | 25 |
| M | Merari | 10 | Madera | 10 | Mesopotamia | 10 | 30 |
| | | | | | | TOTAL FINAL | 55 |

| NAME: Priscilla Smith | | | | | TEAM: In the Beginning | | |
|---|---|---|---|---|---|---|---|
| LETRA | NAME DE PERSONA | points | OBJETO, ANIMAL O PLANTA | points | LUGAR | points | TOTAL |
| E | Elon | 10 | Aves | 10 | Egypt | 5 | 25 |
| M | Manasseh | 10 | ---------------------- | 0 | Moab | 10 | 20 |
| | | | | | | TOTAL FINAL | 45 |

# Crossword Puzzle

## Instructions:

1. Each team is given a crossword puzzle of 6 or 8 questions. Each team is given five minutes to answer. Teams must submit their crossword puzzle in the allotted time.
2. At the end of the five minutes, 10 points are awarded for each correct answer.

## Consultations:

Consultation is only allowed among the 3 participants of the team.

## Foul:

If team members consult with the coach or other children of the team who are not participating, the judge will inform the moderator and the moderator will disqualify the crossword of that team, thereby eliminating their participation in this game only.

## Example:

Three crosswords based on different stories in Genesis are proposed.

## Suggestion:

Since the category is memorization, it is suggested that the proposed crosswords be used in the competition.

### Points
10 points for each correct answer

### Time
5 minutes

### Participants
3 per team

### Mode
Simultaneous

### Materials
- A paper with the same crossword puzzle for each team.
- One pen per team

## Answers:

| CROSSWORD 1 | CROSSWORD 2 | CROSSWORD 3 |
|---|---|---|
| **Across** | **Across** | **Across** |
| 3. wanderer | 2. wood | 3. Benjamin |
| 4. Enosh | 3. Isaac | 5. Goshen |
| 5. farmer | 4. Abraham | 6. five |
| | 6. knife | |
| **Down** | | **Down** |
| 1. offering | **Down** | 1. threehundred |
| 2. shepherd | 1. Moriah | 2. Pharaohs |
| 5. field | 5. angel | 4. ten |

# Crossword puzzle #1

Based on Cain and Abel, Genesis 4

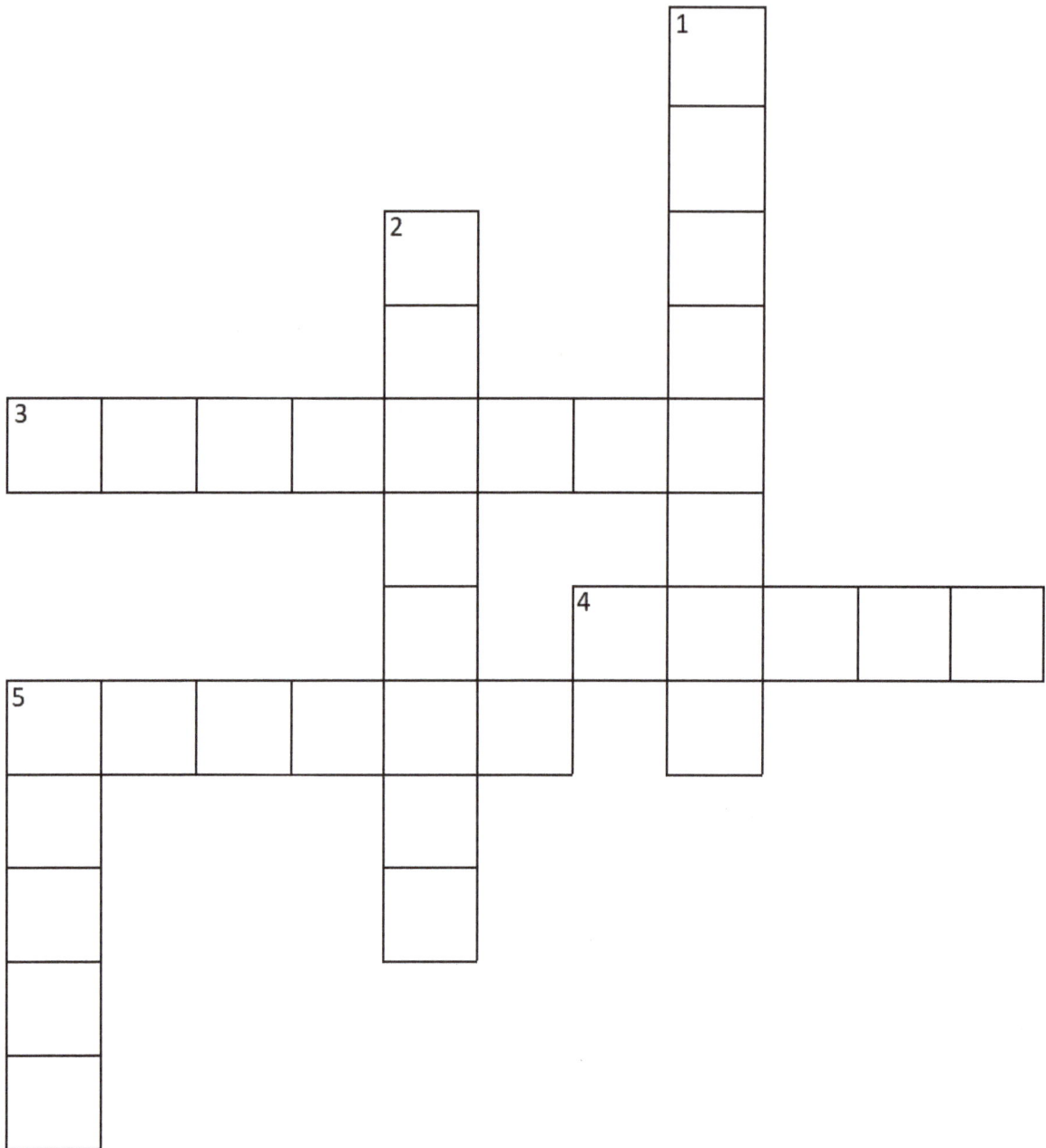

## Across

3. What would Cain be on the earth?
4. What was the name of Cain's son?
5. Cain was a _____

## Down

1. What did the brothers bring to Jehovah?
2. Abel was a _____ of sheep.
5. Cain told his brother Abel to go out to the _____

# Crossword puzzle #2

Based on Abraham and Isaac, Genesis 22

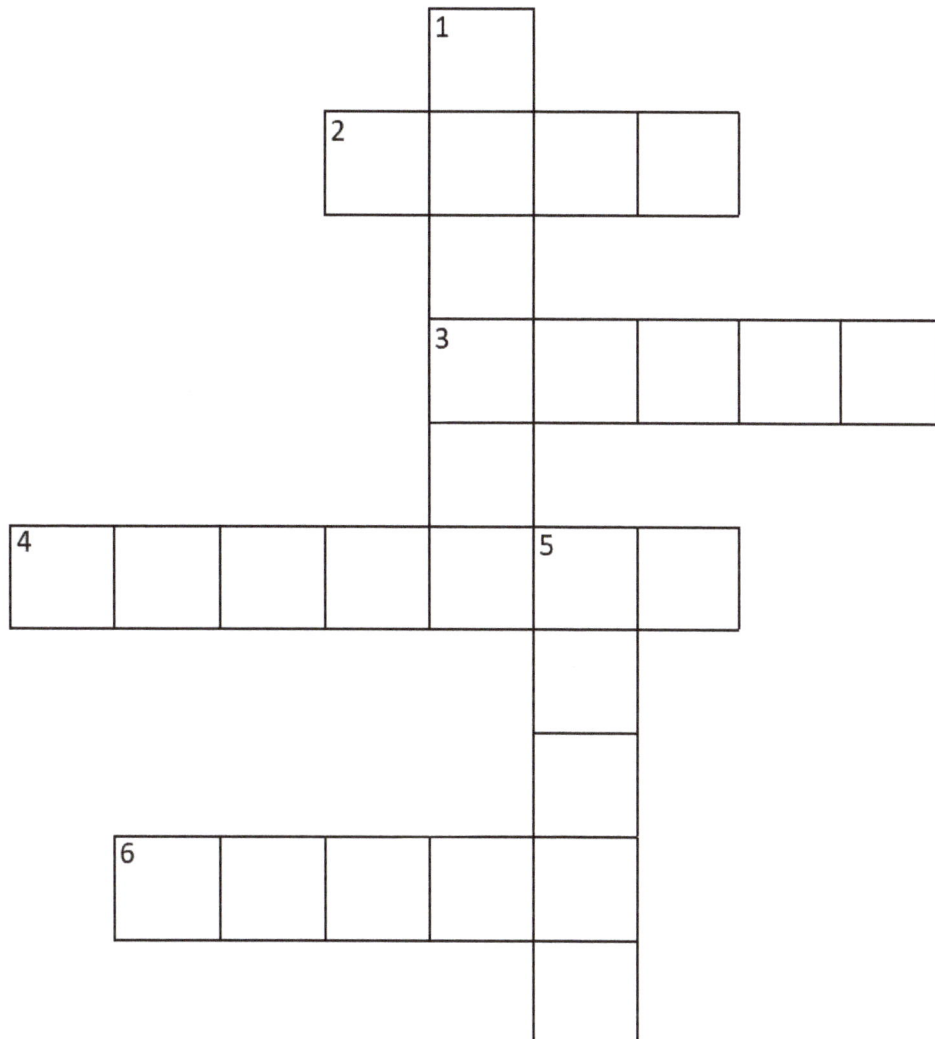

## Across

2. What did Abraham cut for the sacrifice?
3. Who did Abraham love?
4. Who did God want to test?
6. What did Abraham take into his hand?

## Down

1. To what land did God tell Abraham to go?
5. Who stopped Abraham?

# Crossword Puzzle #3

Based on Joseph making himself known - Genesis 45

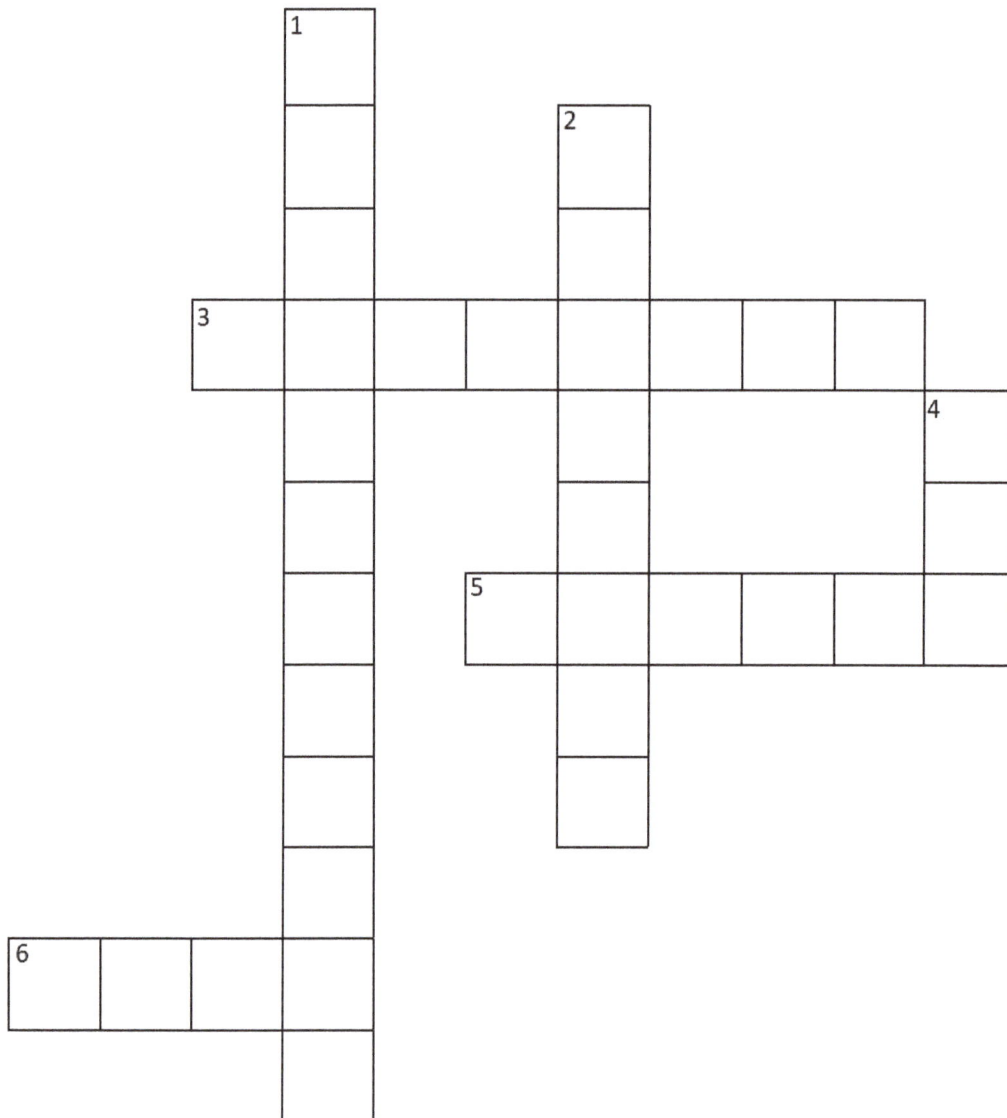

**Across**

3. Who cried as he embraced Joseph?

5. In which land would Joseph's family live?

6. How many years of famine were still to come?

**Down**

1. How many pieces of silver did Joseph give to Benjamin?

2. In whose house was the news of Joseph's brothers heard?

4. How many donkeys loaded with the best of Egypt did Joseph send to his father?

# Answer and Advance

## Instructions:

1. The moderator draws the order of participation, and then attaches on the board or wall a drawing to connect the dots, which must have 15 dots to connect. (see example).
2. The first team to participate stands three meters away from the drawing, one participant behind the other, the moderator allows them to choose an envelope with questions and gives them the markers.
3. The moderator reads the first question, immediately after which the five minutes start counting down. Each participant has 30 seconds to give their answer. If it is correct, they connect two dots with black color. If it is incorrect, they must connect the two dots with red color. Then the participant runs back to their team to hand the markers to the next person in line and the moderator reads the next question.
4. If the participant doesn't respond with the answer within 30 seconds, the judge indicates it, and the participant must draw a red line, and the moderator will say the answer.
5. The time does not stop nor can the questions be repeated.

## Consultations:

Are not permitted

## Foul:

- If one of the participants goes twice in a row, the judge indicates it and cancels a question.
- If one of the participants draws two lines of the drawing, the judge indicates it and cancels a question.
- If someone in the audience says an answer out loud, the judge indicates it and a red line must be drawn.
- Take into account that time does not stop at any time.

## Example:

Following you will find an example of a set of questions and a drawing.

## Points

5 points for each correct answer

## Time

5 minutes

## Participants

2 per team

## Mode

One team at a time

## Materials

- A drawing with 15 points to connect for each team.
- Closed envelopes with sets of 15 questions (different for each team).
- A black marker (correct), and a red marker (incorrect).

# Answer and Advance Set of questions

1. Complete the following verse and give the reference: "So God created mankind in his own image, in the image of God he created them ...
   **Answer: "male and female he created them." (Genesis 1:27)**

2. What was Adam's work in the Garden of Eden?
   **A: Work the land and name the animals. (2:15-20)**

3. Why did God create the woman for the man?
   **A: It wasn't good for the man to be alone. (2:18-20)**

4. From what did God create the woman?
   **A: From one of Adam's ribs (2:21-22)**

5. What did the serpent say to Eve about God's command?
   **A: Did God really say, 'You must not eat from any tree in the garden'? (3:1)**

6. What did the serpent say would happen if the woman ate from the tree in the middle of the garden?
   **A: She would not certainly die, her eyes would be opened, she would be like God, she would know good and evil. (3:2-5)**

7. Who ate the fruit first?
   **A: The woman (3:6)**

8. When did the man and woman realize that they were naked?
   **A: After they ate the fruit (3:6-7)**

9. Why did Adam and Eve hide from God?
   **A: They were afraid because they were naked (3:8-10)**

10. Who did the man blame when God asked him if he had eaten from the tree?
    **A: The woman, Eve (3:11-12)**

11. What happened to the serpent?
    **A: God cursed the serpent. (3:14)**

12. What happened because of Adam and Eve's disobedience?
    **A: God sent them out of the garden, he cursed the earth, and Eve would have more pain in her pregnancies and childbirth. (3:16-19, 23)**

13. Why did Adam call the woman Eve?
    **A: Because she would become the mother of all living things. (3:20)**

14. How did Adam get the garments of skin?
    **A: God made them. (3:21)**

15. With what did God guard the path to the tree of life?
    **A: With cherubim and a flaming sword (3:24)**

# Answer and Advance drawing

11 · · · · 10 · · · · 9

12

13

8 · · · 7

14 6

0 5 4

1 3

2 2

# Discover the Verse

## Instructions:

1. The moderator chooses the order of participation at random.
2. The moderator must prepare as many memory verses as teams that will be participating. The verses must be different for each team, taken from the list of memory verses. The length of the verses chosen should be similar. Cards are presented with one letter of the verse on each card; the cards are to be the size of a quarter piece of letter size paper (4.25 x 5.5 inches) and the letter written proportionally to the size of the card. The cards are to be taped or hung on a board or wall with the letter facing the wall so that the participants can't see the letter. You can number the back side of the cards to locate the letters faster.
3. The participant stands two meters away from the verse and has the opportunity to choose four letters and/or numbers. The moderator will then flip over all the cards that have the chosen letters/numbers. (Similar to the American game show "Wheel of Fortune."
4. The participant has 1 minute to discover the verse. If she is correct, the judge indicates it and 40 points are scored. If she does not discover it or does not say it during the first minute, then she doesn't accumulate any points.

## Consultations:
Are not permitted.

## Foul:
If the participant consults with his team, or someone in the audience says a letter aloud, attention is called to the foul. If the foul is committed again, the judge will cancel the participant's participation in this game.

If the team or a member of the audience says any part of the verse, the participation of the team in this game is canceled.

## Example:

## Points
50 points

## Time
1 minute

## Participants
1 per team

## Mode
One team at a time alternating

## Materials
- Bible memory verses written one letter per card on cards the size of ¼ letter size paper. Different verse for each team.

**Row 1**

| S | O | | G | O | D | | C | R | E | A | T | E | D | | M | A | N | K | I | N | D |
|---|---|---|---|---|---|---|---|---|---|---|---|---|---|---|---|---|---|---|---|---|---|
| 1 | 2 | | 3 | 4 | 5 | | 6 | 7 | 8 | 9 | 10 | 11 | 12 | | 13 | 14 | 15 | 16 | 17 | 18 | 19 |

**Row 2**

| I | N | | H | I | S | | O | W | N | | I | M | A | G | E, | | I | N |
|---|---|---|---|---|---|---|---|---|---|---|---|---|---|---|---|---|---|---|
| 20 | 21 | | 22 | 23 | 24 | | 25 | 26 | 27 | | 28 | 29 | 30 | 31 | 32 | | 33 | 34 |

**Row 3**

| T | H | E | | I | M | A | G | E | | O | F | | G | O | D | | H | E |
|---|---|---|---|---|---|---|---|---|---|---|---|---|---|---|---|---|---|---|
| 35 | 36 | 37 | | 38 | 39 | 40 | 41 | 42 | | 43 | 44 | | 45 | 46 | 47 | | 48 | 49 |

**Row 4**

| C | R | E | A | T | E | D | | T | H | E | M; | | M | A | L | E | | A | N | D |
|---|---|---|---|---|---|---|---|---|---|---|---|---|---|---|---|---|---|---|---|---|
| 50 | 51 | 52 | 53 | 54 | 55 | 56 | | 57 | 58 | 59 | 60 | | 61 | 62 | 63 | 64 | | 65 | 66 | 67 |

**Row 5**

| F | E | M | A | L | E | | H | E | | C | R | E | A | T | E | D | | T | H | E | M. |
|---|---|---|---|---|---|---|---|---|---|---|---|---|---|---|---|---|---|---|---|---|---|
| 68 | 69 | 70 | 71 | 72 | 73 | | 74 | 75 | | 76 | 77 | 78 | 79 | 80 | 81 | 82 | | 83 | 84 | 85 | 86 |

**Row 6**

| G | E | N | E | S | I | S | | 1 | : | 2 | 7 |
|---|---|---|---|---|---|---|---|---|---|---|---|
| 87 | 88 | 89 | 90 | 91 | 92 | 93 | | 94 | | 95 | 96 |

The moderator can use this key to make flipping cards easier, however, one of these must be created for each verse.

| A | 9, 14, 30, 40, 53, 62, 65, 71, 79, | K | 16 | U | —————— |
|---|---|---|---|---|---|
| B | —————————— | L | 63, 72 | V | —————— |
| C | 6, 50, 76, | M | 13, 29, 39, 60, 61, 70, 86 | W | 26 |
| D | 5, 12, 19, 47, 56, 67, 82, | N | 15, 18, 21, 27, 34, 66, 89 | X | —————— |
| E | 8, 11, 32, 37, 42, 49, 52, 55, 59, 64, 69, 73, 75, 78, 81, 85, 88, 90 | O | 2, 4, 25, 43, 46, | Y | —————— |
| F | 44, 68 | P | —————————— | Z | —————————— |
| G | 3, 31, 41, 45, 87 | Q | —————————— | 1 | 94 |
| H | 22, 36, 48, 58, 74, 84, | R | 7, 51, 77, | 2 | 95 |
| I | 17, 20, 23, 28, 33, 38, 92 | S | 1, 24, 91, 93 | 3 | 96 |
| J | —————————— | T | 10, 35, 54, 57, 80, 83 | | |

# Tell Me The Person

## Instructions:

This is a guessing game which is based on people from the book being studied; Each riddle must have three to four clues about a character in the book to be studied.

1. The moderator must have two questions in an envelope for each participating team, with a participation number on the outside. The envelopes are then chosen by the teams.
2. Each participant must answer their question without consulting with his/her teammate. The participant has one minute to give the answer. If the answer is correct, the moderator says "**CORRECT**" and the judges award 20 points to the team (for each correct answer). If the answer is not correct or is not answered in the given time, the participant loses their chance and the moderator gives the correct answer. (No points are awarded to the team.)
3. The moderator continues with a participant from the other team, and alternates between each of the teams until each of the 2 participants from each team have been given the opportunity to answer a question.

## Consultations:

Are not permitted.

## Foul:

If a judge observes that a participant consults with his/her team or someone else present, the moderator will cancel the question and ask a different question. If the participant has already been caught doing this before, the moderator will cancel the question and the team loses its opportunity.

## Example:

### Points
25 points for each correct answer

### Time
1 minute

### Participants
2 per team

### Mode
One team at a time alternating

### Materials
- Envelopes with the clues, two per team and some extras.

# Tell me the Person EXAMPLES OF RIDDLES:

| | | |
|---|---|---|
| I was created with the dust of the earth, Jehovah blew in my nose to give me breath of life and I was created to rule over fish, birds and beasts. Who I am?<br><br>**ANSWER/ ADAM (Genesis 2:7)** | I'm more cunning than any farm animal, I tricked Eve into eating from the tree in the middle of the garden. Who I am?<br><br>**A/ The Serpent (Genesis 3:1-3)** | I am a son of Adam and Eve, my name means "substitute", and I also had a son and I called him Enosh.<br>Who I am?<br><br>**A/SETH (Genesis 4:25-26)** |
| I found grace in the eyes of Jehovah, I was a righteous man, perfect in my generations and I walked with God; My children are Shem, Ham and Japheth.<br>Who I am?<br><br>**A/ NOAH (Genesis 6:9-10)** | Jehovah asked me to leave my land and my people and go to a land that he would show me. I went with Sarai, my wife and my nephew Lot.<br>Who am I?<br><br>**A/ ABRAM (Genesis 12:1-5)** | I am an old woman of advanced age. God kept his promise, I became pregnant, and I gave birth to a son, and I said, "God has brought me laughter."<br>Who I am?<br><br>**A/ SARAH (Genesis 21:1-6)** |
| I came to the well with a water jar on my shoulder, I am Bethuel's daughter and granddaughter of Milkah and Nahor. I gave water to Abraham's servant and camels.<br>Who I am?<br><br>**A/ REBEKAH (Genesis 24:15-19)** | We fought even in our mother's womb; at birth they knew we were twins. I am blond and hairy and my brother was born grabbing my heel.<br>Who are we?<br><br>**A/ JACOB Y ESAU<br>(Genesis 25:19-26)** | I wrestled with Jacob in Peniel until dawn. He asked me to bless him. I changed his name to "Israel" because he had fought with God and with men and won.<br>Who I am?<br><br>**A/ AN ANGEL<br>(Genesis 32:22-28)** |
| I am seventeen years old and I feed the sheep with my brothers. My father loves me more than them because he had me in his old age and made me a robe of different colors<br>Who I am?<br>**A/ JOSEPH (Genesis 37:1-3)** | I rescued Joseph from the hand of our brothers who wanted to kill him. I told them to put him in the cistern that is in the desert<br>Who I am?<br><br><br>**A/ REUBEN (Genesis 37:21-24)** | I didn't want us to kill Joseph our brother, it is our own flesh, but it occurred to me to sell it to the Midian merchants who gave us twenty pieces of silver for him.<br>Who I am?<br><br>**A/ JUDÁ (Genesis 37:26-28)** |
| We are in the same prison where Joseph is in prison. We both had a dream on the same night, each with a meaning and Joseph interpreted them. Who are we?<br><br><br>**A/ THE CUPBEARER AND BAKER<br>(Genesis 40)** | I had a dream and the cupbearer sent for Joseph to interpret it. I didn't find another man with the Spirit of God in him like him; that's why I put him over my house and as governor of my people.<br>Who I am?<br>**A/ PHARAOH (Genesis 41)** | I cried when I embraced Joseph. He gave me three hundred pieces of silver and five changes of clothes.<br>Who I am?<br><br><br>**A/ BENJAMIN<br>(Genesis 45:14-22)** |

# Memory

## Instructions:

1. The moderator randomly chooses the order in which the teams participate.
2. The cards are placed on the floor or on a table face down and scrambled.
3. When given the starting signal, the participants of the first team turn over all the cards and have a maximum of 5 minutes to match up the 8 verses with their biblical references.
4. When all the pairs are connected, or at the end of the time period, the judge reviews the pairs and awards 10 points per correct pair.
5. The cards are scrambled and put back on the floor or table for the next team.
6. The judge must also record the time in which each team connects the 8 pairs. A bonus of 10 points is given to the team that completes all the pairs in the shortest time.
7. The verses must be taken from the list of memory verses.

## Consultations:

The participants cannot consult with their coach or with other members of their team; only among themselves.

## Foul:

If someone from the audience says a verse or reference, the judge will subtract 10 points from the team.

## Points

10 points for each correct pair
10 bonus points for the team that matches all the pairs in the least amount of time

## Time

5 minutes

## Participants

2 per team

## Mode

One team at a time

## Materials

- 16 cards (8 with the biblical texts and 8 with the respective biblical reference) for each team. The texts must be taken from the list of verses to be memorized.

## Example:

| In the beginning God created the heavens and the earth. | GENESIS 1:1 |
| Noah was a righteous man, blameless among the people of his time, and he walked faithfully with God. | GENESIS 6:9b |

# Magic Word

## Instructions:

1. No team may see the puzzle before the competition is started. The game is played simultaneously by all participating teams. Each team will work on a different puzzle, but with the same number of letters. The search starts from the letter with the star, and the participants must draw a line in any direction, even diagonally, to join the letters and find the word. The letter must be adjacent horizontally, vertically, or diagonally to connect. When a participant finds the word, he must write it on the line below the puzzle and have a judge verify it.
2. Once the word puzzles are placed on the wall, blackboard or table, the game is started immediately. No team may see the puzzle before the competition is started.
3. The first participant to correctly discover and connect the letters for the word within the time limit wins. The judges must record the time that each puzzle is completed in case there is a disagreement of who finished first. If there is a tie, 10 points is awarded to each team. If a participant incorrectly does their puzzle, the judge who checks it indicates that it is incorrect, and the team is immediately disqualified, and the game continues with the rest of the participants.
4. If none of the teams discover the word, no team receives points.

## Consultations:
Are not permitted.

## Foul:
If anyone present says the word aloud, the judge will indicate it. This game is void, and no team gets points. The game is restarted with a new word game for each team if extra puzzles are available.

## Words to play:
5 letters = Babel, Jacob, Sarai, Isaac, Egypt, knife
6 letters = Canaan, Rachel, Reuben, camels
7 letters = Abraham, Gomorra, Promise, Rebekah, Pharaoh, Japheth, Jehovah, Shechem, Lentils
8 letters = Benjamin, Gomorrah, Potiphar

## Example:

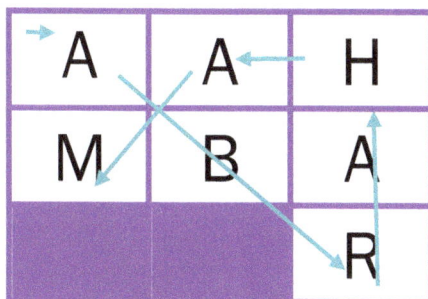

Abraham

Benjamin

### Points
20 points

### Time
1 minute

### Participants
1 per team

### Mode
Simultaneous

### Materials
- A puzzle with the word to decipher for each team (plus a few extras).
- A marker or pen/pencil for each team

# The Key Letter

## Instructions:

The moderator will give a sealed envelope that will contain a category (characters, places, objects, animals, miscellaneous) and a base vowel to each participating team. The teams will participate simultaneously by writing a list of words related to the selected category containing the specific base letter they received in their envelope.

1. Each team will choose an envelope containing a category and base letter from the moderator.
2. The 3 participants will form a line three meters away from the board. When the moderator gives the signal, the first participant of each team goes to the board and writes a qualifying word, then returns to their team and hands the marker/chalk to the next participant of his team.
3. That second participant then goes to the board and writes the second word and so on until the time limit of one minute is over.

## NOTE:

The participant can run or walk to and from the board.

## Consultations:

Are not permitted.

## Foul:

If the judge observes that the participants of a team are speaking among themselves, the value of a word is deducted. If someone from the audience says a word in a loud voice, a judge will indicate it and the value of a word is deducted from all teams.

## Example:

### Points

5 points for each correct word

### Time

1 minute

### Participants

3 per team

### Mode

Simultaneous

### Materials

- Sealed envelopes that contain a category (characters, places, objects, animals, miscellaneous) and a base vowel for each participating team

- Chalk boards, white boards, or large pieces of paper - enough for all teams to write on at the same time.

- A marker/chalk for each team

### PERSON "A"

```
        A
    C a i n
E s a u
    A d a m
    R a c h e l
    J a c o b
    S a r a h
```

### PLACE "E"

```
        E
        E d e n
        E g y p t
    P e n i e l
S e c h e m
G o s h e n
```

# Alphabet Soup

## Instructions:

Each team will receive the same puzzle at the same time.

Each team must discover the words that appear horizontally, vertically, diagonally, top to bottom, left to right or vice versa.

1. The moderator places the puzzles face down on the table or floor in front of each team. The puzzles must have in the title a topic related to the search, for example: Creation, Joseph and his brothers, etc.

2. When the start signal is given, each team must turn over the puzzle and find the words. Words must be circled and written down on the side of the puzzle.

3. When a team finishes, they must take their completed puzzle to one of the judges for review (the time is recorded). (The other teams continue working on their puzzles.) If the judge observes that the team has found all of the correct words, he/she will inform the moderator. The competition stops and one of the participants reads the list aloud and that team wins 50 points.

4. If the word puzzle is incorrect on some word(s), the judge will simply say "Incorrect" and the team will continue to search for words

The maximum time for this competition is 7 minutes. If no team finishes during the set time, the competition is scored according to the correct answers (5 points per correct answer).

## Consultations:

Consultation on the puzzle will only be between the two participants of the team.

## Foul:

If a participant consults with someone other than their other participating teammate, the judge will indicate it and give them a 30-second penalty.

## Points

5 points for
each correct word

## Time

7 minutes

## Participants

2 per team

## Mode

Simultaneous

## Materials

- A marker or pencil per team.
- Word-search puzzles with ten words to discover – sufficient number for each participating team to receive one copy.

## Answers:

| ALPHABET SOUP 1 | ALPHABET SOUP 2 | ALPHABET SOUP 3 |
|---|---|---|
| Heaven | Isaac | Joseph |
| Earth | Jacob | Donkeys |
| Seas | Esau | Cup |
| Day | Rebekah | Money |
| Night | Stew | Wheat |
| Light | Hairy | Benjamin |
| Animals | Firstborn | Brothers |
| Seeds | Blessing | Canaan |
| Plants | Clothes | Silver |
| Man | Goats | Clothes |

# ALPHABET SOUP 1

## Based on the creation, Genesis 1

| H | E | A | V | E | N | P | A | N | V | R | E | C | T | B |
|---|---|---|---|---|---|---|---|---|---|---|---|---|---|---|
| Q | U | I | Z | I | Y | U | M | I | H | E | Q | U | J | Q |
| H | H | N | C | L | E | F | S | T | I | V | O | L | A | E |
| D | O | O | U | A | T | I | R | R | R | S | D | E | E | S |
| L | A | M | M | N | D | A | M | O | L | A | G | N | I | A |
| J | I | Y | O | B | E | L | I | R | A | A | O | U | T | R |
| E | K | M | B | N | R | S | L | E | A | N | T | E | C | E |
| P | L | M | A | E | R | E | L | C | B | I | I | R | M | R |
| L | L | I | G | H | T | U | A | I | A | M | L | A | I | B |
| A | A | A | R | C | H | G | A | T | R | A | O | M | L | M |
| N | T | U | S | V | G | S | R | T | O | L | T | I | O | U |
| P | A | A | A | S | I | E | H | C | O | S | A | E | S | L |
| A | P | L | A | N | T | S | S | O | T | I | E | L | A | A |
| S | P | A | N | I | M | A | N | E | S | C | M | A | N | L |
| I | S | A | B | U | L | Y | A | L | V | I | R | U | Z | E |

1.
2.
3.
4.
5.
6.
7.
8.
9.
10.

# ALPHABET SOUP 2

Based on Jacob getting Isaac's blessing, Genesis 27

| I | C | A | E | L | G | U | I | S | A | N | T | I | L | O |
|---|---|---|---|---|---|---|---|---|---|---|---|---|---|---|
| O | L | Y | J | A | C | O | B | A | G | G | O | A | T | S |
| D | O | A | J | A | B | O | R | R | U | A | L | A | B | A |
| N | T | S | D | B | E | N | D | I | C | I | O | N | U | G |
| I | H | R | O | N | L | A | S | D | I | E | Z | Y | S | N |
| I | E | G | T | Y | S | T | E | W | R | R | L | S | E | I |
| S | S | C | V | B | D | J | S | B | E | E | A | O | U | S |
| A | I | E | R | O | V | J | A | E | B | B | S | D | Q | S |
| A | P | T | Y | S | D | O | U | C | Y | E | O | I | A | E |
| R | H | U | I | E | T | T | U | O | L | K | N | T | L | L |
| E | A | A | L | I | I | H | K | D | E | A | C | S | A | B |
| B | L | A | I | E | B | E | C | S | A | H | E | E | J | M |
| C | A | B | R | R | M | N | R | O | B | T | S | R | I | F |
| O | A | B | E | N | Y | E | C | I | O | N | D | I | D | I |
| C | F | U | I | I | S | A | A | C | U | L | L | E | V | R |

| |
|---|
| 1. |
| 2. |
| 3. |
| 4. |
| 5. |
| 6. |
| 7. |
| 8. |
| 9. |
| 10. |

75

# ALPHABET SOUP 3

Based on Joseph's Cup in a Sack, Genesis 44

| | | | | | | | | | | | | | |
|---|---|---|---|---|---|---|---|---|---|---|---|---|---|
| C | O | O | P | A | A | V | B | N | M | N | A | S | D | F |
| A | R | T | E | C | V | S | E | O | I | R | E | Y | E | R |
| H | E | R | M | O | G | E | R | M | R | A | R | J | S | T |
| C | O | P | A | C | V | E | A | I | E | U | G | N | Y | G |
| L | R | B | E | N | V | J | A | P | G | C | A | V | E | B |
| O | E | E | W | L | N | O | C | M | A | U | S | A | K | V |
| T | N | N | I | H | T | J | O | S | E | P | H | O | N | H |
| H | I | S | B | R | E | R | S | F | O | V | D | P | O | E |
| E | D | A | R | T | I | A | T | C | V | I | Z | I | D | R |
| S | C | L | T | E | G | V | T | T | T | D | A | U | R | M |
| O | O | O | P | P | H | A | L | S | V | O | S | H | E | A |
| T | M | R | A | L | E | T | N | I | M | A | J | N | E | B |
| F | T | N | L | A | R | V | O | E | D | T | R | I | G | O |
| C | A | Y | E | N | O | M | H | R | R | M | I | O | V | S |
| C | C | A | N | A | A | N | V | E | B | T | L | L | R | U |

| |
|---|
| 1. |
| 2. |
| 3. |
| 4. |
| 5. |
| 6. |
| 7. |
| 8. |
| 9. |
| 10. |

# Finish The Story

## Instructions:

The moderator will have a list of biblical passages to read, one for each participating team. The biblical passages must be different, but they must have the same number of verses.

1. The moderator draws the order of participation.

2. The 3 participants of the first team will sit in the three chairs. The moderator begins by reading the biblical passage to the first team. As soon as one of the three participants of the team recognizes the passage, they must interrupt the moderator by rising from their place to continue the story. The time begins the moment the moderator starts reading and stops when the participant gets up. The judges record this time. The moderator instructs the participant to finish the story. The participant has 1 minute to do so.

3. When the participant finishes the story, the moderator announces if the rest of the story is correct or not, and the time obtained. If the story is not correct, the moderator announces "INCORRECT." If 2 or 3 participants of the team get up at the same time, they must immediately decide which participant will continue.

4. The moderator then repeats the process with a different passage for the next team.

5. The winning team is the one who correctly finishes the story and has the shortest time elapsed during the reading of the moderator. The time judge must make sure that the participant does not exceed the 1-minute time limit to complete the story.

## Consultations:

Quiet consultation between the 3 participants of the team is allowed.

## Foul:

If one of the participants gets up from his place to finish the story, but forgets the rest of the story, he is given 15 seconds to start his response. If he remains silent or sits down again, the judge indicates "INCORRECT" to the moderator, ending the participation of that team in this game.

## Stories:

- Disobedience of man, 3:1-13
- The promise of Isaac's birth, 18:1-15
- God commands Abraham to sacrifice Isaac, 22:1-13
- Jacob and Esau, 25:19-34
- Joseph is sold by his brothers, 37: 23-36
- Joseph interprets Pharaoh's dreams, 41: 17-30
- Joseph's cup in the sack, 44: 4-17

## Points

50 points

## Time

1 minute

## Participants

3 per team

## Mode

One team at a time

## Materials

- One biblical passage for each team. Each passage must be different, but the same number of verses.
- Three chairs

# REFLECTION CATEGORY

The coach facilitates the lesson considering the objective or purpose of the teaching, and dialogues with the children of the team allowing them to formulate their questions. The objective of this category is to motivate the boys and girls to reflect on the Bible reading in terms of the spiritual teachings it contains, and the context (historical, cultural, idiomatic, etc.) in which it is developed.

Let children know that learning is the result of personal effort.

SOME REFLECTION TECHNIQUES:

- Dialogue
- Directed Questions
- Active listening and intense participation
- Focus on the essentials
- Harmonize theory and practice

For a local, district, zone, national demonstration, etc. the moderator will choose:

# 2 reflection games

The teams will find out which games will be played only on the day of the demonstrations.

# Chest Of Memories

## Instructions:

The moderator will place the objects inside the chest/trunk/box beforehand.

1. Each team will choose a participation number.

2. Starting with team 1, the moderator will invite the first participant to put his hand into the chest and take out an object without looking. The participant then will have 2 minutes to explain what that object represents from the Bible verses being studied.

3. If the participant relates his story well, the judge will give him 10 points, and then continue on to the second participant of the same team. The same directions apply to the second participant, as well as to additional teams. Each participant can earn 10 points, for a maximum of 20 points per team.

## NOTE:

An object that has been taken out of the chest is not put back in after the participant is finished with it.

## Consultations:

Are not permitted.

## Foul:

If a participant consults with his partner or anyone else, the judge will deduct 10 points from the team.

## Example:

**Points**

20 points for explaining correctly

**Time**

2 minutes

**Participants**

2 per team

**Mode**

One team at a time

**Materials**

- Objects of any material
- A wooden chest or trunk, or one made out of cardboard
- Participation numbers

| Tree | Chapt. 1, 2, 3 | Lentils | 25:34 |
|---|---|---|---|
| Seeds | Chapt. 1 | Cup | Chapt. 40, 44 |
| Animals | Chapt. 1, 7, 8 | Wheat | Chapt. 41-45 |
| Wood | 6:14 | Cows | Ch. 41, 45:10 |
| Brick | Chapt. 11 | Carts | Chapt. 45, 46 |
| Knife | Chapt. 22 | Robe | Chapt. 37 |
| Firewood/wood | Chapt. 22 | Angel | 28:12, 32:22 |
| Camels | Chapt. 24 | Stars | Ch. 1, 15, 37 |
| Jar/Pitcher | Chapt. 24 | Sand | Ch. 22, 32, 41 |

# Mailbox

## Instructions:

1. Each team will choose a participation number.
2. Ask one of the participants from the first team to put their hand in the mailbox and randomly choose a letter, which will have characteristics of a biblical character to discover.
3. The moderator will read the letter that was chosen, and as soon as the reading is finished, the team will have 1 minute to discuss and agree on which biblical character the letter is written to. Then only one of the participants will tell the moderator the identity of the biblical character.
4. If the team choses correctly, the judge scores 20 points. If their answer is incorrect, they receive zero points.

## Consultations:

The team participants can only talk among themselves; they cannot consult with their coach.

## Foul:

If someone from the audience or another team speaks at the time of the response, the judge indicates this and deducts 10 points from the team incurring the foul.

## Example:

**Points**

50 points

**Time**

1 minute after the reading

**Participants**

The whole team

**Mode**

One team at a time

**Materials**

- Letters with characteristics of biblical characters (different for each team).
- A mailbox, can be of any material.

**Letter 1**

Hello, I hope you are very well, I am writing to you because I learned that God asked you to leave your land and your people and go to Canaan, I am glad to know that you are not going alone, that you are with your wife, one of your nephews and the people you acquired in Haran. You will surely go through Bethel and then to the Negev. Maybe we will find each other on the road, take care. **Answer: Abram**

**Letter 2**

Dear friend, I hope everything goes well, I am writing this letter to ask you to greet your grandparents Milkah and Nahor, I send greetings to Bethuel your father, I have a lot of time not to see you, but they have told me that you look beautiful, remember to always carry your jug when you go to the fountain, one of these days we meet there and give the camels a drink. **Answer: Rebekah**

# How Do You Imagine It?

## Instructions:

1. The moderator has the participants choose a random envelope.
2. The moderator opens the envelope of the first participant and reads the place, and the child has a minute to give the name of the event that happened in that place and a description of what he imagines that place was like.
3. The judge evaluates both the name of the event and the description of the place according to the study book. If both are correct, the team receives 30 points.
4. If the participant only says what event happened in the place, 10 points are recorded. If the participant does not respond during the minute, the points are not recorded and the moderator gives the answer.

## Consultations:

Are not permitted.

## Foul:

If the child consults with the coach or with other members of his team or if someone in the audience says something out loud, the judge indicates it and that person's participation in this game is forfeited.

**Points**

30 points

**Time**

1 minute

**Participants**

1 per team

**Mode**

One team at a time

**Materials**

- One envelope per team with a place name where an important event happened.

## Places:

| PLACE | EVENT | DESCRIPTION |
|-------|-------|-------------|
| Eden, chapt. 2-3 | Jehovah planted a garden there and put man there to take care of it. | Allow the children to use their imagination to describe what these places were like. |
| A plain in Shinar, chapt. 11 | The people built a tower with bricks, Jehovah confused their language and called that place Babel. | |
| Water well, chapt. 24 | Rebekah gave a drink of water to Abraham's servant and camels. | |
| Peniel, chapt. 32 | Jacob fought with an angel until daybreak, his name was changed to Israel. | |

# Bible Bingo

(This is similar to the popular game BINGO, using words instead of numbers, and one must fill up the whole card, not just a row.)

The moderator will prepare ½ or ¼ page sized game cards with 9 squares drawn on them for each participant (see next page for an example). Each square will have 1 word in it. All of the words will be different words taken from the scripture passage to be read by the moderator. 8 out of the 9 words will be different than all of the other words on all of the other game cards that all of the other participants have. However, the 9th word in each group will contain the same word – it will be the last word of the biblical passage. (Look at the example on the next page.) You can see that every word on every game card is different except the key word, which is the last word of the passage, which is "GROUND."

1. When it is time to start, each participant will place their game card and small game pieces in front of themselves on the table, and familiarize themselves with the words on their game card.

2. The moderator will begin to read the chosen biblical passage. (The passage must be no shorter than ten verses and cannot last for more than 3 minutes.) While the moderator reads, the participants must listen carefully to the reading. When the moderator reads a word that is written on a participant's game card, that participant will place one of their game pieces on their game card. (Similar to the game BINGO.)

3. Whoever correctly fills her/his game card first and yells out "FINISHED" will receive 30 points for their team.

NOTE: If there is a tie between teams, 30 points will be awarded to each team. If there is a tie between 2 participants of the same team, only 30 points are given. If at the end of the passage reading, no participant has completely filled their card, nobody gets points.

## CONSULTATIONS:
Not permitted.

## FOUL:
If a team interrupts or asks questions during the reading, the judge will take away 2 points from that team.

## SUGGESTION OF BIBLICAL PASSAGES
- Cain y Abel - 4:1-10
- Jacob fights with the angel at Peniel - 32:22-32
- Joseph's dreams - 37:1-11

## Points
30 points

## Time
However long the moderator takes in reading the biblical passage.

## Participants
2 per team

## Mode
Simultaneous

## Materials
- Selected Bible passage
- 2 Game cards for each team
- 9 small objects for each participant that will be used as game pieces or markers (beans, corn, buttons, bottle caps, plastic disks, etc.)

# Example of game cards:

These examples of game cards are based on the biblical passage of "Cain and Abel", in this case the key word is "ground".

| | | |
|---|---|---|
| ADAM | LORD | FLOCKS |
| FIELD | GROUND | FAT |
| ACCEPTED | BROTHER | ATTACKED |

| | | |
|---|---|---|
| CAIN | ANGRY | FRUITS |
| FACE | SIN | FIELD |
| GROUND | KEEPER | ADAM |

| | | |
|---|---|---|
| GROUND | ABEL | EVE |
| SOIL | OFFERING | DOWNCAST |
| DOOR | FIRSTBORN | RULE |

| | | |
|---|---|---|
| MAN | ACCEPTED | FAVOR |
| FAT | EVE | GROUND |
| KEEPER | KILLED | SIN |

# Statements (NEW GAME)

## Instructions:

1. The moderator places the game cards on the table or floor, face down, in front of each team participants.
2. When given the start signal, the participants will turn over their game card and will have 1 minutes to link the places or characters with the statements and write them in the spaces provided.
3. At the end of Time, the teams give their game cards to the judge. 5 points are awarded per correct box.

## Consultations:

Only between the two participants from the team.

## Foul:

If the participants try to see the responses of another team, the judge points it out and their participation in this game is forfeited.

## Example:

**Points**

5 points for each correct box

**Time**

1 minute

**Participants**

2 per team

**Mode**

Simultaneous

**Materials**

- One game card for each team (same card for all).
- A pen for each team.

| The serpent | Adam | Eve | Noah |
|---|---|---|---|

| | | |
|---|---|---|
| He was more crafty than any of the wild animals.<br><br>*The Serpent* | We can eat fruit from the trees of the garden. | He named every beast and bird under heaven. |
| Both were naked. | He found grace in the eyes of Jehovah. | Mother of all living things. |
| He did everything that Jehovah commanded him. | You will crawl on your belly and you will eat dust | He lived 930 years and then he died. |

84

# Two Edged Sword

## Instructions:

1. The moderator has each participant choose a random envelope with 3 questions inside and a participation number on the outside.
2. The moderator reads the questions from the envelope to the participant of the first team. The child must answer if it is false or true. To do this, they will have 1 minute after the moderator begins reading the first question.
3. If the participant does not answer correctly, the moderator will say the correct answer and read the next question.
4. The judge will give 10 points for each correct answer.

## Note:

It must be taken into account that time does not stop once the moderator has begun reading the first question.

## Consultations:

Are not permitted.

## Foul:

If the participant consults with his team or a member of the audience says one of the answers aloud, the judge indicates it and their participation in this game is forfeited.

## Points

10 points for each correct answer

## Time

1 minute

## Participants

1 per team

## Mode

One team at a time alternating

## Materials

- Envelopes with three different questions for each team.

## Example:

**Envelope 1**

1. The children of Eve mentioned in Genesis are Shem, Ham and Japheth. True or False?
   **A/ False (4)**

2. The offering that pleased Jehovah was that of Abel. True or False?
   **A/ True (4:4)**

3. The person who killed Cain would be punished 10 times. True or False?
   **A/ False (4:15)**

**Envelope 2**

1. The Lord said it would rain forty days and forty nights. True or False?
   **A/ True (7:4)**

2. Noah was 700 years old when he entered the ark. True or False?
   **A/ False (7:11, 13)**

3. The sons of Noah were Shem, Cain, and Jacob. True or False?
   **A/ False (6:10)**

# Order Of Events

## Instructions:

1. The moderator will put five scenes of a story into a sealed envelope with a participation number on the outside. He will prepare as many stories as there are teams to participate. The story must be different for each team.

2. When the moderator gives the start signal, each participant will have 2 minutes to put their story scenes into the correct order according to how the biblical event happened. At the end of the time (2 minutes), the moderator will give each participant 1 minute to tell the story, going in order of the participation number on the outside of their envelopes.

3. 50 points will be given for putting the story scenes into the correct order, and 10 points for telling the story correctly, for a maximum total of 60 points per team.

## Note:

It is best to have the story scenes on 5 separate pieces of paper or cards so that the participants can move them around to put them into the correct order instead of just having all of the scenes on the same piece of paper.

## Consultations:

Are not permitted.

## Foul:

Consultation with the coach or anyone else is prohibited, and will result in disqualification of the team for this game.

## Example:

Based on "The Fall" 3:1-13
(Images taken from hermanamargarita.com)

## Points

60 points (50 for correct order and 10 for telling the story)

## Time

3 minutes (2 to put in order and 1 to tell the story)

## Participants

1 per team

## Mode

Simultaneous for putting in order and one at a time to tell the story.

## Materials

- Stories from Genesis divided in 5 scenes.

# Follow The Footprints

## Instructions:

1. All teams will choose an envelope from the moderator and then line up at the START in front of the giant footprints on the floor.
2. The moderator will receive the envelope from team #1 and ask a question from the questions inside to the participant from team #1. The participant has 30 seconds to give the answer. If in 30 seconds they correctly answer the question, they put their color card on the first footprint. If they don't give the correct answer or remain silent, the moderator will say the correct answer and they won't be able to advance.
3. Then the moderator will receive the envelope from the second team and ask that team's participant the first question from that list, and so forth through the teams.
4. Once all teams have been asked question 1, the moderator begins again with team #1 by asking their question #2 and so forth. When a team answers correctly, they advance their colored card marker along the footprints. When a team answers incorrectly, they don't move their colored card marker.
5. The game is over after 12 questions have been asked to each participant. Teams that answer all 12 questions correctly will reach footprint #12 and receive 60 points. All other teams will receive 5 points for each correct answer they give.

## Consultations:

Are not permitted.

## Foul:

If someone from the audience says the answer aloud, 10 points will be deducted from the team that committed this infraction.

## Example:

### Points

5 points for each correct answer

### Time

30 seconds to give the answer

### Participants

1 per team

### Mode

One team at a time alternating

### Materials

- The moderator will prepare a questionnaire with 12 different questions for each team and put it in a sealed numbered envelope.
- 12 FOOTPRINTS made of any material
- 2 signs, one that says "START," the other "FINISH,"
- a different colored card for each team.

Isabel from Team "Genesis" correctly answered 9 questions earning 45 points for her team.

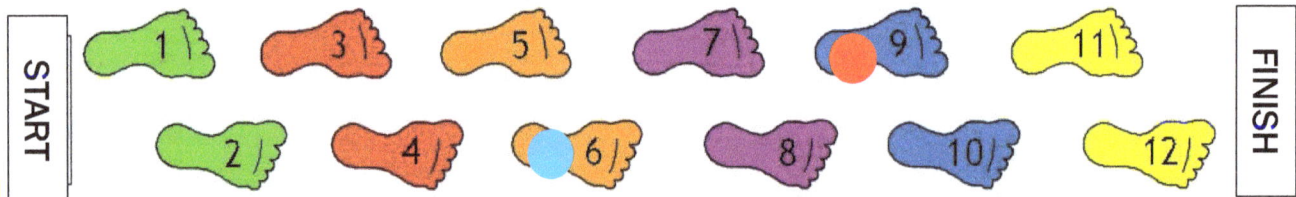

Raymond from Team "In the Beginning" correctly answered 6 questions earning 30 points for his team.

# ARTS & CRAFTS CATEGORY

Arts and Crafts can also be used as teaching tools, helping the children with their personal creativity development, as well as a form of recreation. They are used in the early stages of learning because they help with the development of gross and fine motor skills.

This category will help the children represent biblical knowledge through different arts and crafts expressions.

**IDEAS:**

- Ask your local SDMI president to supply you with teaching materials, paper of different colors and textures, scissors, glue, yarn, glitter, straws, finger paint, paints, brushes, etc.

- Do activities that allow children to develop their creativity.

For a local, district, zone, national demonstration, etc. the moderator will choose:

# 1 Arts and Crafts game

The teams will know the game that will be played only on the day of the demonstration.

# Flags

## Instructions:

1. Each team will receive an envelope and materials to create their flag. When the moderator gives the signal, each team will have 5 minutes to create a flag that somehow illustrates the place or character that they received in their envelope.

2. At the end of 5 minutes, all teams will stop working. Then one participant from each team will have 1 minute to explain their flag. This will be done according to their participation number.

The judges will award points based on the following criteria:

- Quality of workmanship and creativity: 5-10 points
- Explanation: 5-10 points
- Good use of the materials: 5-10 points

## Consultations:
Only among the participants of the team.

## Foul:
If during the explanation, a different participant or a member of the audience speaks, 10 points will be deducted from the team that commits this infraction.

## SUGGESTION OF PLACES:

- Eden, Chapt. 2-3
- Mt. Ararat, Chapt. 8
- Shinar, Chapt. 11
- Moriah, Chapt. 22
- Peniel, Chapt. 32
- Joseph's Prison, Chapt. 39-42

## Points
30 points

## Time
5 minutes to make the flag and 1 minute to explain it

## Participants
2 per team

## Mode
Simultaneous - all teams participate at one time making their flags, and one team at a time explaining them

## Materials

- The moderator will prepare 1 card per team, on which is written the name of a place or Bible character from the biblical passages being studied. Each card must be different. These cards are placed in sealed envelopes with a participation number on the outside.

- Sheets of paper, colored paper, wooden or plastic sticks of 60 cm. White glue, scissors, markers.

# Collage

## Instructions:

1. The moderator will have each team choose an envelope with a theme and participation number.

2. Each team will be given materials and a place to make their collage.

3. The moderator will start the game with a whistle – all teams will participate at the same time. Each team will have 5 minutes to make a collage to illustrate the theme that they received in their envelope. Team members may talk with one another, but not with anyone else.

4. After 5 minutes, all teams will stop working on their collages. Each team will appoint a representative from among the three, who will have 1 minute to explain their collage. Teams will present in the order of their participation number.

**THE JUDGES WILL AWARD POINTS BASED ON THE FOLLOWING CRITERIA:**

- Creativity and good use of colors: 5-10 points
- Use of materials: 5-10 points
- Explanation: 5-10 points

## Consultations:

Talking only among the 3 participants of the team.

## Foul:

5 points will be deducted from the team that is talking to each other during the explanation of the collages by any of the participating teams.

## Suggestion Of Themes:

- Cain and Abel, 4:1-10
- The Flood, 7:1-10
- The Tower of Babel, 11:1-9
- Isaac and Rebekah, 24:61-67
- Jacob fights with the angel at Peniel, 32:22-32
- Joseph's dreams, 37:1-11

## Points

30 points

## Time

5 minutes to make the collage
1 minute to explain it.

## Participants

3 per team

## Mode

Simultaneous - all teams participate at one time to make their collages, and then 1 team at a time will explain their collage.

## Materials

The moderator will prepare 1 theme for each team in sealed envelopes, with the participation number on the outside.

Cardboard or letter-sized paper, scissors, white glue, paper of different colors and textures, such as tissue paper, newspaper, etc.

# Answer And Draw

## Instructions:

1. The moderator will give each team an envelope containing the base drawing, as well as a theme story and 5 different questions about that story. The envelopes will be numbered on the outside.
2. When it is time for the first team to start, the team will hand their envelope to the moderator, who will tape the base picture to a board or wall that the team can easily reach to draw on.
3. The team will form a line in front of the base drawing with the 5 participants. The moderator will announce their theme story, and then ask the first participant a question from the envelope. When the moderator finishes the first question, the time of 1 minute is started per participant. If the participant answers the question correctly, he will start drawing on the base picture, illustrating the theme story that they have been given. He draws until his minute is up. If the participant answers incorrectly, he does not proceed to draw on the picture, his turn is over, and the moderator continues by asking the next team participant a question. If that participant answers the question correctly, he goes and continues the same drawing that the first person started, and so forth. After all 5 participants of the team have had the opportunity to answer a question and draw, the moderator will ask a team representative to explain the picture they drew (1 minute time limit).
4. After the first team finishes, the moderator moves on to the second team, and so forth.

### The judges award points based on these criteria:
- Clarity of the drawing: 5-10 points
- Drawing is relevant to the subject of study: 5-10 points
- The picture is drawn realistically: 5-10 points

## Consultations:
Not permitted.

## Foul:
If another participant answers the question asked to their teammates or if someone else answers out loud, the participation of this team is canceled for this game only.

## Suggestion Of Themes:
- Cain and Abel, 4:1-10
- The Flood, 7:1-10
- The Tower of Babel, 11:1-9
- Isaac and Rebekah, 24:61-67
- Jacob fights with the angel at Peniel, 32:22-32
- Joseph's dreams, 37:1-11

## Points
30 points

## Time
3 minutes

## Participants
5 per team

## Mode
One team at a time

## Materials
- The moderator will present a base drawing, such as a prison, city, mountains, sea, etc., on a sheet of paper for each team to draw on. The drawing must be different for each team.
- Colored markers for the team drawing.

# Emotion-Art

## Instructions:

This game was designed with the understanding that the coach of each team should be teaching the children about emotions and how to manage them.

1. The moderator chooses numbers for the order of the teams.

2. Each participant is given a paper with two silhouettes of faces (male/female) and a marker.

3. The moderator will say the name of a character(s) and an event in which the character(s) felt some emotion. For example: "Paul in the Shipwreck."

4. Each participant must draw the facial expressions that correspond to the emotion that the character felt, in this case, the drawing would be done on the male silhouette. They will have 1 minute to do this. (In case you talk about several characters such as guards, church, etc., they can use both silhouettes).

5. After the minute of drawing, according to the order that was drawn, each participant will give an explanation to the judges about the emotion and why they think the character felt it.

For this game, the following evaluation scale will be used:
- Clarity and quality of the drawing: 5-10 points
- Explanation: 5-10 points

## Consultations:

Are not permitted.

## Foul:

If a participant tries to see or replicate what another team is doing, the judge indicates it and their participation in this game is canceled.

## Suggestion of Themes:
- Adam and Eve leave the Garden of Eden, 3:23-24
- Noah, when God established his covenant with him, 9:8-13
- People when God confused their language, 11:7-9
- Isaac upon seeing that he was going to be sacrificed by his father, 22:9-10
- Joseph at being sold by his brothers, 37:28
- Joseph's brothers upon seeing that Benjamin had the cup, 44:1-17
- Joseph and his brothers when he introduced himself, 45:9-14

### Points
20 points

### Time
1 minute to draw,
1 minute to explain

### Participants
1 per team

### Mode
Simultaneous - all teams participate at one time drawing, and one at a time explaining

### Materials
- Papers with silhouettes of faces (man / woman) (2 silhouettes per team)
- Markers

| | | | |
|---|---|---|---|
|  angry |  confused |  disappointed |  disgusted |
|  |  |  |  |

 happy

 innocent

 lonely

| | | | |
|---|---|---|---|
|  nervous |  peaceful |  proud |  sad |

afraid

shocked

sick

joking

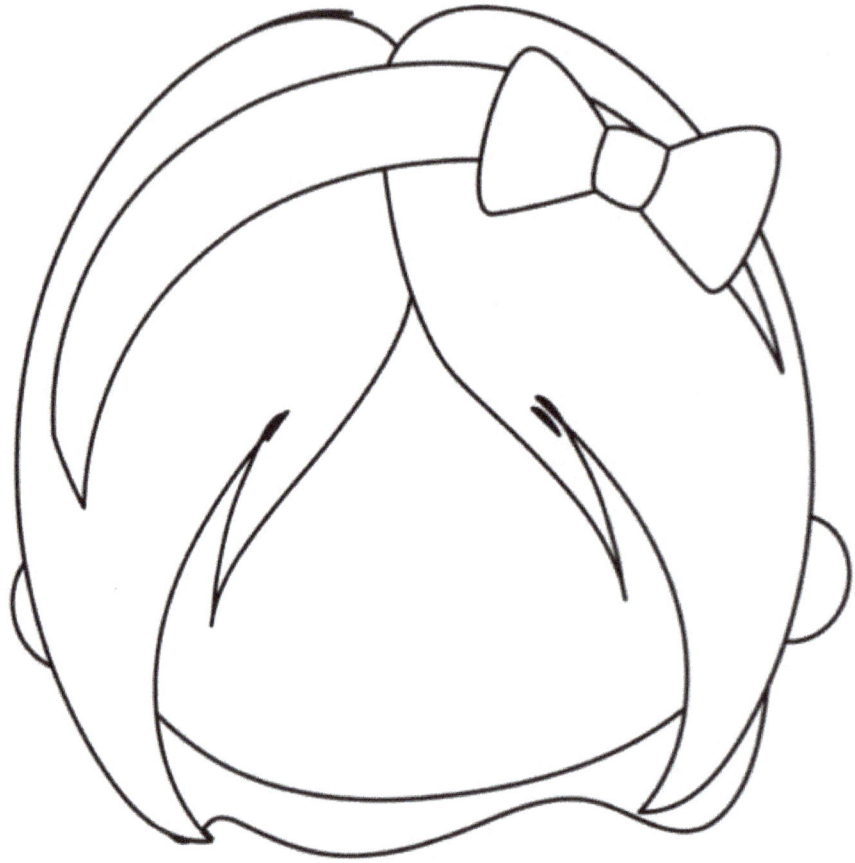

# Puppets

## Instructions:

1. The moderator will ask the two participants of each team to sit on the floor or at a table, along with their envelope and supplies.

2. When the moderator blows his whistle, each team will create a puppet that represents their Bible character. At the end of 5 minutes, all the teams must stop working. Then in order of participation number, 1 member from each team will have 1 minute to use their puppet to explain who they are.

**The judges will award points based on the follow criteria:**
- Creativity and workmanship of the puppet: 5-10 points
- Creativity in the presentation: 5-10 points
- Good use of the materials: 5-10 points

## Consultations:

Consultations permitted only between the 2 members of the team.

## Foul:

5 points will be deducted from teams that talk during the explanation of their character or while other teams are presenting.

## Note:

At the end of the activity, an exhibition can be made to appreciate the work the children did and to reward their creativity.

## Suggested Characters:

- Adam
- Ev3
- Noah
- Abraham
- Isaac
- Jacob
- Sarah
- Rebekah
- Joseph
- Benjamin

### Points

30 points

### Time

5 minutes to make the puppet, 1 minute for the presentation

### Participants

2 per team

### Mode

Simultaneous - all teams participate at one time making the puppets, and one team at a time for the presentations

### Materials

- The moderator will prepare an envelope for each team with the name of the Bible character the team needs to portray and a participation number on the outside. This Bible character must be different for each team.
- Paper bag, white glue, paper of different textures and colors wool or yarn, markers, scissors for each team.

# ACTING CATEGORY

The game consists in representing a character in an integral way. For this it is necessary that the actor, the child, knows the character and can express it with his body expressions and voice.

In this category, the objective is to develop in the child the ability to express with his body a spiritual message that involves the study of the Word of God.

**SOME IDEAS:**

- Create an atmosphere of respect and a positive spirit in the children so that they do not mock or laugh when one of their classmates participates in this category.

- Perform activities that allow the children to gain self-confidence and lose shyness.

For a local, district, zone, national demonstration, etc. the moderator will choose:

# 1 performance game

The teams will know the game that will be done only on the day of the demonstration.

# Poetry

## Instructions:

1. Each team will receive a participation number. The moderator starts with the first team to participate, giving one minute for the 2 participants to present their poem together.

The judges will award points based on the following criteria:

- Gestures                                          5-10 points
- Coordination between the 2
  members of the team                    5-10 points
- Intonation                                      5-10 points
- Lyrics                                             5-10 points
- Content related to the study theme    5-10 points

Note: The poem must have 3 stanzas and the presentation must be no longer than 1 minute. It must have been written by the team, and have unpublished lyrics.

## Consultations:

Are not permitted.

## Foul:

5 points will be deducted from a team that is talking when another team is making its presentation.

## Example:

They shine, they shine, hundreds of stars!
Look at the skies now and count each one of them
God made them with his voice like a poem
All are totally beautiful.

They shine, they shine, hundreds of stars!
Look at the skies now and count each one of them
As you can count them that way, your offspring will be
Thank you Lord for your great radiance

They shine, they shine, hundreds of stars!
Look at the skies now and count each one of them
I enthusiastically pick up your sweet promises
Through me the whole earth will be blessed.

## Points

50 points

## Time

1 minute

## Participants

2 per team

## Mode

One team at a time

## Materials

# Charades

## Instructions:

1. The moderator will write down a theme/Bible story on note cards, a different one per team, and put them in sealed envelopes with participation numbers on the outside. The envelopes must not be opened until it is time for the team to participate.

2. The participant who chooses the envelope must act out the theme/Bible story so that his 4 remaining teammates can try to guess the theme/Bible story he is trying to communicate through his actions. The team has 2 minutes to give the correct answer.

3. The judge awards 25 points if the team answers correctly. If the team answers incorrectly, the judge indicates it and no score is given to that team. The moderator should say the correct answer out loud if it is not guessed.

## Consultations:

Only among the 4 participants who must guess the theme.

## Foul:

If anyone in the audience or other members of a team interrupt by saying possible answers, the judge indicates it and the moderator cancels the team's participation in this game only.

## Suggestion Of Themes:

- Cain and Abel, 4:1-10
- The Flood, 7:1-10
- The Tower of Babel, 11:1-9
- The statue of salt, 19:24-26
- Isaac and Rebekah, 24:61-67
- Jacob fights with the angel at Peniel, 32:22-32
- Joseph's dreams, 37:1-11

## Points
25 points

## Time
2 minutes

## Participants
5 per team

## Mode
One team at a time

## Materials
- 1 envelope for each team with their theme (different for each team) participation number

# Drama

1. Each team will choose an envelope.

2. With all teams starting at the same time, the moderator will give the go ahead, and the teams will have 5 minutes to prepare their dramas with the themes that they received in their envelopes. The drama should be presented as if it were happening today in modern times.

3. After the 5 minutes of preparation time, coaches must leave and the teams must present their dramas in the order of their participation numbers. Once team #1 has finished, team #2 will begin, etc....

Note: It's important to take into account that teams must bring their costumes, decorations and other props they wish to use with them to the demonstration.

### The judges will award points based on the following criteria:

- Participation of the whole team: 5-10 points
- The ability to represent the story accurately: 5-10 points
- The fluidity of the dialogue: 5-10 points
- Use of available resources (props, decorations, etc.): 5-10 pts
- The drama is faithful to the teaching of the event/theme: 5-10 pts

## Consultations:
During the first 5 minutes, they can consult with the coach and among themselves. During the presentation, coaches cannot be consulted.

## Foul:
10 points will be deducted from a team if they speak during another team's presentation

## Suggestion Of Themes:
- The Fall, 3:1-13
- The Promise of Isaac's Birth, 18:1-15
- God tells Abraham to sacrifice Isaac, 22:1-13
- Jacob and Esau, 25:19-34
- Joseph is sold by his brothers, 37:23-36
- Joseph interprets Pharaoh's dreams, 41:17-30
- Joseph's cup, 44:4-17

## Points
50 points

## Time
5 minutes

## Participants
The whole team

## Mode
Simultaneous - all teams participate at one time preparing their dramas, and one team at a time presenting

## Materials
- The moderator will write down a biblical event on cards, a different one for each team, and then place them in sealed envelopes with participation numbers on the outside.

# Breaking News

## Instructions:

1. Each team will choose an envelope.

2. When the moderator gives the go ahead, the teams will have 3 minutes to prepare their news report about the event they received in their envelope. After the 3 minutes of preparation time, one of the team participants will have 1 minute to present the news report as informatively, creatively and interestingly as possible.

3. Once team #1 has finished, team #2 will begin.

**The judges will award points based on the following criteria:**

- Creativity                                          5-10 points
- Content related to the study theme     5-10 points
- Fluidity of the dialogue                       5-10 points

## Consultations:

Only permitted among the 4 participants during the first 4 minutes. In addition, they can consult their Bibles.

## Foul:

Ten points are deducted from a team that is talking to each other while another team is presenting.

## Suggestion Of Themes:

- Adam and Eve expelled from the Garden of Eden, 3:23-24
- God makes a covenant with Noah, 9:8-13
- Confusion of languages at the Tower of Babel, 11:7-9
- Lot's wife turned into a statue of salt, 19:24-26
- Isaac is going to be sacrificed by his father, 22:9-10
- Joseph is sold by his brothers, 37:28
- Benjamin is found with Joseph's cup, 44:1-17

## Points

30 points

## Time

4 minutes

## Participants

4 per team

## Mode

All teams will prepare their newscast at the same time, and then one team at a time will present

## Materials

- The moderator will put a biblical event or bible passage on note cards, a different one for each team, and then place them in sealed envelopes with participation numbers on the outside.

- Letter size piece of paper and pencil or pen for each team.

# MUSIC CATEGORY

Music is the art of organizing sounds in a sensible and coherent way, with harmony, melody and rhythm. The objective of this category is to teach the child to praise God intelligently, doing so with the knowledge of God's Word, with a biblical foundation and spiritual knowledge.

## IDEAS:

- Ask for help from members of the worship ministry.
- Provide small times of praise in your meetings with the team.
- Identify the children with skills on instruments or a good singing voice.
- Allow children to participate in the creation of an unpublished song, thus develop their creativity.

For a local, district, zone, national demonstration, etc. the moderator will choose

# 1 music game

The teams will know the games that will be played only on the day of the demonstration.

As for the unpublished song, this must be presented in the final demonstration.

# Sing The Verse

## Instructions:

1. Each team will choose an envelope with their Bible verse and participation number.

2. When the moderator gives the start signal for the first team to start, the team will have 3 minutes to read the verse and then come up with a tune and choreography. The team will then present the "song."

**The judges will award points based on the following criteria:**

- Intonation and harmony:       5-10 points
- Creativity in the presentation: 5-10 points

## Consultations:
The team can consult with their coach during the first 3 minutes.

## Foul:
If a team talks while another team is presenting, 10 points will be deducted from the team that commits this infraction.

## Suggestion Of Texts:
Choose a text from the Memory Verse list found on page 65.

## Points
20 points max.

## Time
3 minutes

## Participants
The whole team

## Mode
One team at a time

## Materials

- The moderator will prepare a card for each team with Bible verses from the memory verse list (a different one for each team) and put them in sealed envelopes with participation numbers on the outside.

# New Song

## Instructions:

Each team must present an unpublished song, which will be sung by the whole team. The team can present it with choreography or spiritual dancing, etc. The song must have:

- Unpublished lyrics (lyrics must be written by the team)
- Lyrics related to the theme of Bible Quizzing.
- The actual tune may be from a published Christian song, but the lyrics must be changed.
- Minimum of two verses, maximum of four.
- Maximum duration of three minutes.

1. The moderator will draw the order of participation.
2. Each team will have a maximum of 3 minutes to present their song, ideally with music, and actions.

**The judges will award points based on the following criteria:**

- Quality of the Unpublished lyrics: 5-10 points
- Lyrics related to the theme of the Quizzing Study: 5-10 pts
- Music (intonation, harmony): 5-10 points
- Creativity in the presentation: 5-10 points
- Full team participation: 5-10 points

## Consultations:

Are not permitted.

## Foul:

20 points will be deducted from a team that is talking while another team is presenting.

## Points

50 points

## Time

3 minutes

## Participants

The whole team

## Mode

One team at a time

## Materials

# Musical Roulette

## Instructions:

1. The moderator draws the order of participation and places the roulette in front of the spectators.

2. The participants make a line in the order of participation three meters away from the roulette wheel.

3. Each child will rotate the wheel and according to the character that the wheel stops at, he will have a maximum of 1 minute to sing a small musical jingle. (These musical jingles should be prepared in advance with the help of the coach.)

**The judges will award points based on the following criteria:**

Music (intonation, harmony): 5-10 points

Creativity in the presentation: 5-10 points

## Consultations:

Are not permitted

## Foul:

Ten points are deducted from a team if it is talking while another team is presenting.

## Suggestions Of Characters

- Adam
- Eve
- Noah
- Abraham
- Isaac
- Jacob
- Sarah
- Rebekah
- Joseph

### Points

20 points

### Time

1 minute

### Participants

1 per team

### Mode

One team at a time

### Materials

- Roulette of Characters

# ACTIVITIES FOR TEACHING MEMORY VERSES

## BIBLE VERSE FUN

Ask the children to sit in a straight line. Tell the first child to stand, to say the first word of the verse, to wave both hands excitedly in the air, and to sit down. Ask the second child to stand, to say the second word of the verse, to wave both hands excitedly in the air, and to sit down.

Continue until the verse is complete. If a child forgets a word or says the wrong word, let the other children tell the correct word. Encourage the children to say the verse quickly so that their motions look like an ocean wave.

## BIBLE PASS

You will need a Bible and a source of music for this activity.

Have the children sit in a circle. Give one child the Bible. When the music starts, tell the children to pass the Bible around the circle.

When the music stops, the child holding the Bible says the Bible verse. Tactfully stop the music so each child has an opportunity to say the verse.

## BIBLE VERSE RACE

Write each word or phrase of a Bible verse on a piece of paper. Make two sets, one for each team.

Divide the class into two teams. Place a set of word cards on the floor in front of each team. Scramble the order of the cards. After a signal, let the first child on each team find the first word of the verse and run to a goal line.

The child places the card on the floor and races back to the second player. That child picks up the second word of the verse and races with it to the goal line. Continue until one team completes the verse in perfect order. Allow time for the second team to complete its verse. Then have both teams recite the verse together.

## BIBLE VERSE LINE UP

Write each word or phrase of a Bible verse on a piece of paper.

Give each child a verse card. Instruct the children with cards to go to different parts of the room and hold up the card. Choose another child to line up the children in the correct order of the verse. Then have the class read the verse together.

## HIDE AND SEEK MEMORY GAME

Prepare papers and hide them in advance for this activity.

Write each word of the memory verse on a separate piece of paper. Hide the individual words around the room. Ask the children to find the words and to arrange them in the correct order. Recite the memory verse.

## STAND UP VERSES

Instruct the children to sit in a circle. Instruct the first child to stand and say the first word of the verse, and then he or she sits down. The second child stands and says the second word of the verse, and then he or she sits down. Continue until the children complete the verse. Encourage the children to play again, but to go faster than the previous time. Let the children see how quickly they can say the verse.

## MISSING WORDS MEMORY GAME

You will need a chalkboard, marker board, or paper for this activity.

Write the memory verse on a chalkboard or marker board. Ask the children to recite the verse. Permit a child to erase one word, and then ask the children to repeat the verse (including the missing word.) Continue until all the words disappear, and the children say the verse from memory. If a chalkboard or marker board is not available, write each word of the verse on a separate piece of paper, and ask the children to remove one word at

# MEMORY VERSES

"In the beginning God created the heavens and the earth." Genesis 1:1

"So God created mankind in his own image, in the image of God he created them; male and female he created them." Genesis 1:27

Then the Lord God said to the woman, "What is this you have done?" The woman said, "The serpent deceived me, and I ate." Genesis 3:13

"Noah was a righteous man, blameless among the people of his time, and he faithfully walked with God." Genesis 6:9b

"As long as the earth endures, seedtime and harvest, cold and heat, summer and winter, day and night will never cease." Genesis 8:22

"I have set my rainbow in the clouds, and it will be the sign of the covenant between me and the earth." Genesis 9:13

"Do not be afraid, Abram. I am your shield, your very great reward." Genesis 15:1b

"Look up at the sky and count the stars—if indeed you can count them." Then he said to him, "So shall your offspring be." Genesis 15:5b

But Lot's wife looked back, and she became a pillar of salt. Genesis 19:26

"Because you have done this and have not withheld your son, your only son, I will surely bless you." Genesis 22:16b-17a

When the time came for her to give birth, there were twin boys in her womb. Genesis 25:24

That night the Lord appeared to him and said, "I am the God of your father Abraham. Do not be afraid, for I am with you; Genesis 26:24a

"I am with you and will watch over you wherever you go, and I will bring you back to this land. I will not leave you until I have done what I have promised you." Genesis 28:15

Then the man said, "Your name will no longer be Jacob, but Israel, because you have struggled with God and with humans and have overcome." Genesis 32:28

Now Israel loved Joseph more than any of his other sons, because he had been born to him in his old age; and he made an ornate robe for him. Genesis 37:3

"I cannot do it," Joseph replied to Pharaoh, "but God will give Pharaoh the answer he desires." Genesis 41:16

"But God sent me ahead of you to preserve for you a remnant on earth and to save your lives by a great deliverance." Genesis 45:7

"But God will surely come to your aid and take you up out of this land to the land he promised on oath to Abraham, Isaac and Jacob." Genesis 50:24b

children'squizzing

# GUIDE FOR CHILDREN'S BIBLE QUIZZING USING QUESTIONS AND ANSWERS

Children's Bible Quizzing is an optional part of Bible Studies for Children. Each church and each child decides whether to participate in a series of competitive events.

Quizzing events follow the rules outlined in this book. Children do not compete against each other to determine a single winner. Churches do not compete against each other to determine a winner.

The purpose of Quizzing is to help the children to determine what they learned about the Bible, to enjoy the competitive events, and to grow in the ability to display Christian attitudes and Christian behaviors during competitive events.

In Quizzing, each child challenges himself or herself to attain an award level. In this approach, children quiz against a base of knowledge, not against each other. Quizzing uses a multiple-choice approach that allows every child to answer every question. Multiple choice questions offer several answers, and the child chooses the correct one. This approach makes it possible for every child to be a winner.

## QUIZZING SUPPLIES

Each child uses a quiz box (see picture) (or similar device) to answer questions during events. The quiz box contains four tab inserts that are numbered 1, 2, 3, and 4. The numbers represent possible answer choices. Participants pull one numbered insert to indicate the correct answer. Children can also use the quiz box to answer multiple-choice review questions in the classroom. The quiz box dimensions are 30 cm wide X 13 cm deep X 28 cm high. Quiz boxes may be purchased from The Foundry (*www.gokidsquiz.com),* or a local team may make their own. For instructions to make quiz boxes, visit *kidzfirstpublications.net*

Each group of children will need a person to score their answers. There is a reproducible score sheet at the end of the book. Use this score sheet to keep track of the answers of each child.

If possible, provide some type of an award for the performance of the children in each Quizzing event. Suggested awards are certificates, stickers, ribbons, trophies, or medals.

Please follow these rules. Competitions that do not operate in accordance with the Children's Quizzing Official Competition Rules and Procedures will not qualify for other competition levels.

## AGES AND GRADES

Children in grades 1-6 may participate in Children's Quizzing competitions. Seventh graders, regardless of age, participate in Teen Quizzing. (For countries other than the United States, grades 1-6 are generally ages 6-12).

## BASIC LEVEL COMPETITION

This competition level is for younger or beginning quizzers. Older quizzers who prefer an easier level of competition may also participate in the Basic Level. The questions for the Basic Level are simpler. There are three answers for each question, and there are fifteen questions in each round. The district or regional Children's Quizzing director determines the questions and the number of rounds at each Quizzing competition. Most competitions have two or three rounds. (These are found after each chapter of the Bible Study earlier in the book.)

## ADVANCED LEVEL COMPETITION

This competition level is for older quizzers or experienced quizzers. Younger quizzers who want a greater challenge may participate in the Advanced

Level. The questions for the Advanced Level are more comprehensive. There are four answers for each question, and there are twenty questions in each round. The district or regional Children's Quizzing director determines the questions and the number of rounds at each Quizzing event.

## SWITCHING BETWEEN LEVELS

Children may switch between Basic Level and Advanced Level only for invitational Quizzing competitions. This helps the leaders and the children determine the best level for each child.

For the zone/area, the district, and the regional competitions, the local director must register each child for either Basic Level or Advanced Level. The child must compete at the same level for zone/area, district, and regional competitions.

## TYPES OF COMPETITION

### Invitational Competition

An invitational competition is between two or more churches. Local Children's Quizzing directors, zone/area Children's Quizzing directors, or district Children's Quizzing directors may organize invitational competitions. Individuals who organize an invitational competition have the responsibility to prepare the competition questions.

### Zone/Area Competition

Each district may have smaller groupings of churches that are called zones. If one zone has more quizzers than another zone, the district Children's Quizzing director may separate or combine the zones to create areas with a more equitable distribution of quizzers. The term area means combined or divided zones.

The churches located in each zone/area compete in that zone/area. The district Children's Quizzing director organizes the competition. Questions for the zone/area competitions are official questions.

E-mail ChildQuiz@nazarene.org to request these questions from the General Children's Quizzing Office.

### District Competition

Children advance from the zone/area competition to the district competition. The district Children's Quizzing director determines the qualifications for the competition and organizes the competition.

Questions for district competitions are official questions. E-mail ChildQuiz@nazarene.org to request these questions from the General Children's Quizzing Office.

### Regional Competition

The regional competition is a competition between two or more districts.

When there is a regional Children's Quizzing director, he or she determines the qualifications for the competition and organizes the competition. If there is not a regional director, the participating district directors organize the competition.

Questions for the regional competitions are official questions. To request these questions from the General Children's Quizzing Office, e-mail ChildQuiz@nazarene.org.

## WORLD QUIZ COMPETITION

Every four years, the General Children's Quizzing Office in conjunction with Sunday School and Discipleship Ministries International sponsors an international World Quiz. The Global Children's Quizzing Office determines the dates, the locations, the costs, the qualifying dates, and the overall qualifying process for all World Quiz competitions.

E-mail ChildQuiz@nazarene.org for more information.

## DISTRICT CHILDREN'S QUIZZING DIRECTOR

The district Children's Quizzing director operates all competitions according to the Children's Quizzing Official Competition Rules and Procedures.

He or she has the authority to introduce additional Quizzing procedures on the district as long as the procedures do not conflict with the Children's Quizzing Official Competition Rules and Procedures. The district Children's Quizzing director contacts the General Children's Quizzing Office, when necessary, to request a specific change in the Children's Quizzing Official Competition Rules and Procedures for a district. The district Children's Quizzing director makes the decisions and solves the problems within the guidelines of the Children's Quizzing Official Competition Rules and Procedures. The district Children's Quizzing director contacts the General

Children's Quizzing Office for an official ruling on a specific situation, if necessary.

## REGIONAL CHILDREN'S QUIZZING DIRECTOR

The regional Children's Quizzing director creates a regional Children's Quizzing leadership team that consists of all of the district Children's Quizzing directors on the region. The regional Children's Quizzing director remains in contact with this team to keep the procedures consistent across the region. He or she operates and organizes the regional competitions according to the Children's Quizzing Official Competition Rules and Procedures. The regional Children's Quizzing director contacts the General Children's Quizzing Office to request any changes in the Children's Quizzing Official Competition Rules and Procedures for a specific region. He or she resolves any conflicts that arise with the help of the guidelines of the Children's Quizzing Official Competition Rules and Procedures. The regional Children's Quizzing director contacts the General Children's Quizzing Office for an official ruling on a specific situation, if necessary. He or she contacts the General Children's Quizzing Office to place the regional quiz date on the general church calendar.

In the United States and Canada, the regional Children's Quizzing director is a developing position. Currently that person does not preside over district Children's Quizzing directors on the region.

## QUIZMASTER

The quizmaster reads the competition questions at a Quizzing competition. The quizmaster reads the question and the multiple-choice answers two times before the children answer the question. He or she follows the Children's Quizzing Official Competition Rules and Procedures established by the General Children's Quizzing Office and the district Children's Quizzing director/regional coordinator. In the event of a conflict, the final authority is the district/regional Children's Quizzing director who consults the Children's Quizzing Official Competition Rules and Procedures. The quizmaster may participate in discussions with scorekeepers and the district/regional Children's Quizzing director about a challenge. The quizmaster may call a time-out.

## SCOREKEEPER

The scorekeeper scores a group of children's answers. He or she may participate in discussions with scorekeepers and the district/regional Children's Quizzing director about a challenge. All scorekeepers are to use the same method and the same symbols to insure correct tabulation of the scores.

### SYNOPSIS OF HOW THE QUESTIONS ARE READ AND ANSWERED

The quizmaster reads the question and all answer choices twice. After the quizmaster reads the second time, he or she will call the children to respond. The quizmaster never reads questions once.

- The quizmaster says, "QUESTION" and then reads the question and all answer choices.

- The quizmaster repeats this sequence.

- The quizmaster says, "ANSWER," which prompts the participants' to respond.

Example: The quizmaster says, **"QUESTION: What did Mary name her baby? Answer number one, Joseph. Answer number two, John. Answer number three, Jesus."** The quizmaster briefly pauses and starts again and says, **"QUESTION: What did Mary name her baby? Answer number one, Joseph. Answer number two, John. Answer number three, Jesus."** The quizmaster briefly pauses and calls for the answer and says, **"ANSWER."** The children then indicate their answer choice by removing the number from their box that corresponds to their answer.

The quizmaster *may* read a question a third time for especially difficult or long questions or if a mistake was made when the question was initially read. However, this practice should be the exception, and the participants should be notified of a third repeat in advance to avoid premature responses after the second question and answer sequence.

After the answers are indicated, the quizmaster pauses and watches for the scorekeepers to record all the scores. When the scores are recorded, the quizmaster instructs the children to return their answer numbers to their boxes.

For bonus questions, the quizmaster instructs the team representatives who will answer the bonus question for each team to stand and all the other children to place their hands in their laps. The quizmaster reads the question two times. The child who is ready to answer the bonus question steps to the scorekeepers and quietly gives their answer. The child speaks carefully and quietly so that they do not reveal their answer to other teams. When everyone completes their answer, the quizmaster asks the scorekeepers to raise their hand to reveal who correctly answered. The quizmaster affirms the correct answer or invites a participant to share the correct answer.

When possible, use PowerPoint or other visual media to project questions onto a screen that is visible to all quizzers.

The projected presentation will only include the questions. All answers will be read.

## OFFICIAL COMPETITION QUESTIONS

The district Children's Quizzing director is the only individual on the district who may obtain a copy of the official zone/area and district competition questions.

The regional Children's Quizzing director is the only individual on the region who may obtain a copy of the official regional competition questions. If there is not a regional Children's Quizzing director, one participating district Children's Quizzing director may obtain a copy of the official regional competition questions.

Order forms for annual official questions will be sent by E-mail each year. Contact the General Children's Quizzing Office at ChildQuiz@nazarene.org to update your E-mail address. The official questions will arrive by Email to the people who request them.

## COMPETITION METHODS

There are two methods of competition.

### Individual method

In the individual method of competition, the children compete as individual children. The score of each child is separate from all other scores. Children from the same church may sit together, but do not add together the individual scores to obtain a church or a team score. There are no bonus questions for individual quizzers.

The individual method is the only method to use for the Basic Level competition.

### Combination Method

The combination method combines individual and team Quizzing. In this method, churches may send individual quizzers, the teams, or a combination of these to a competition.

The district Children's Quizzing director determines the number of children needed to form a team. All teams must have the same number of quizzers. The recommended number for a team is four or five children.

The children from the churches that do not have enough quizzers to form a team can compete as individual quizzers.

In the combination method, teams qualify for bonus questions. The bonus points awarded for a correct answer to a bonus question become part of the total score of the team, instead of a score for an individual quizzer. There are bonus questions with the official questions for zone/area, district, and regional competitions. Bonus questions typically involve the recitation of a memory verse.

The district Children's Quizzing director selects either the individual method or the combination method for the Advanced Level of the competition.

## TIE SCORES

Ties between individual quizzers or the teams remain as tied scores. All individual children or teams who tie receive the same recognition, the same award, and the same advancement to the next level of competition.

## BONUS QUESTIONS

Bonus questions are part of the Advanced Level, but only with teams, not individuals. Teams must qualify for a bonus question. Bonus questions occur after questions 5, 10, 15, and 20.

To qualify for a bonus question, a team may have only as many incorrect answers as there are members on the team. For example, a team of four members may have four or fewer answers that are incorrect. A team of five members may have five or fewer answers that are incorrect.

The bonus points for a correct answer become part of the total score of the team, not of the individual score of a child.

The district Children's Quizzing director determines the way that the children answer bonus questions. In most situations, the child verbally gives the answer to the scorekeeper.

Prior to the reading of the bonus question, the local Children's Quizzing director selects one team member to answer the bonus question. The same child may answer all of the bonus questions in a game, or a different child may answer each bonus question.

## TIME-OUTS

The district Children's Quizzing director determines the number of time-outs for each church. Each church receives the same number of time-outs, regardless of the number of individual quizzers or teams from that church. For example, if the district director decides to give one time-out, each church receives one timeout.

The district Children's Quizzing director determines if an automatic time-out will occur during the game and the specific point at which the time-out will occur in each game.

The local Children's Quizzing director is the only individual who may call a time-out for a local church team.

The district Children's Quizzing director or quizmaster may call a time-out at any time.

The district Children's Quizzing director, prior to the start of the competition, determines the maximum length of the time-outs for the competition.

## SCORING

There are two methods for scoring. The district Children's Quizzing director selects the method.

### Five Points

• Award five points for every correct answer. For example, if a child answers 20 questions correctly in an Advanced Level round, the child earns a total of 100 points.

• Award five points for every correct bonus answer in an Advanced Level team Quizzing round. For example, if every member of a team with four

persons answers 20 questions correctly in an Advanced Level round and the team answers four bonus questions correctly, the team earns a total of 420 points. Basic Level points will be lower as there are only 15 questions per round, and it is individual competition only.

### One Point

Award one point for each correct answer as follows:

• Award one point for every correct answer. For example, if a child answers 20 questions correctly in an Advanced level round, the child earns a total of 20 points.

• Award one point for every correct bonus answer in an Advanced Level team Quizzing round. For example, if every member of a team with four persons answers 20 questions correctly in an Advanced Level round and the team answers four bonus questions correctly, the team earns a total of 84 points.

Basic Level points will be lower as there are only 15 questions per round, and it is individual competition only.

## CHALLENGES

Challenges are to be an exception and are not common during a competition.

Request a challenge only when the answer marked as correct in the questions is actually incorrect according to the Bible reference given for that question. Challenges issued for any other reason are invalid.

A quizzer, a Children's Quizzing director, or any other competition participant may not request a challenge because they dislike the wording of a question or answer or think a question is too difficult or confusing.

The local Children's Quizzing director is the only person who may issue a challenge to a competition question. If an individual other than the local Children's Quizzing director attempts to issue a challenge, the challenge is automatically ruled as "invalid."

Individuals who issue invalid challenges disrupt competition and cause the children to lose their concentration. Individuals who consistently issue invalid challenges or create some problems by arguing about a challenge ruling will lose their privilege of challenging the questions for the remainder of the competition.

The district Children's Quizzing director, or the quizmaster in the absence of the district Children's Quizzing director, has the authority to remove the privilege of challenging questions from any or all individuals who abuse the privilege.

The district Children's Quizzing director determines how to challenge a competition question prior to the start of the competition.

• Will the challenge be written or verbal?

• When can a person challenge (during a game or at the end of a game)?

The district Children's Quizzing director should explain the procedure for the challenges to local Children's Quizzing directors at the beginning of the quiz year.

The quizmaster and district Children's Quizzing director follow these steps to rule the challenge.

• Determine if the challenge is valid or invalid. To do this, listen to the reason for the challenge. If the reason is valid, the answer given as the correct answer is incorrect according to the Bible reference, follow the challenge procedures outlined by the district.

• If the reason for the challenge is invalid, announce that the challenge is invalid, and the competition continues.

If more than one person challenges the same question, the quizmaster or district Children's Quizzing director selects one local quiz director to explain the reason for a challenge. After a question has one challenge, another person may not challenge the same question.

If a challenge is valid, the district Children's Quizzing director, or quizmaster in the director's absence, determines how to handle the challenged question. Select one of the following options.

**Option A:** Eliminate the question, and do not replace it. The result is that a game of 20 questions becomes a game of 19 questions.

**Option B:** Give every child the points he or she would receive for a correct answer to the challenged question.

**Option C:** Replace the challenged question. Ask the quizzers a new question.

**Option D:** Let the children who gave the answer that was listed as the correct answer in the official questions keep their points. Give another question to the children who gave an answer that was an incorrect answer.

## AWARD LEVELS

Children's Quizzing has the philosophy that every child has an opportunity to answer every question, and every child receives recognition for every correct answer he or she gives. Therefore, Children's Quizzing uses multiple-choice competition, and ties are never broken.

Children and churches do not compete against each other. They compete to reach an award level. All of the children and all of the churches who reach the same award level receive the same award. Ties remain as tied scores.

Recommended Award Levels:

Bronze Award = 70-79% correct

Silver Award = 80-89% correct

Gold Award = 90-99% correct

Gold All Star = 100% correct

Resolve all scoring and challenge decisions before presenting awards. The quizmaster and scorekeepers should be sure that all final scores are accurate prior to the presentation.

Never take an award from a child after the child receives an award. If there is a mistake, children may receive a higher award but not a lower award. This is true for individual awards and team awards.

## COMPETITION ETHICS

The district Children's Quizzing director is the person on the district who has the responsibility to conduct the competitions in accordance with the Children's Quizzing Official Competition Rules and Procedures.

• *Hearing Questions Before the Competition*. Since competitions use the same questions, it is not appropriate for the children and the workers to attend another zone/area, district, or regional competition prior to their participation in their own competition of the same level. If an adult Quizzing worker attends another competition, the district Children's Quizzing director may choose to disqualify the church from participation in their competition. If a parent and/or child attends another competition, the district Children's Quizzing director may choose to disqualify the church from participation in their competition.

• *Worker's Conduct and Attitudes.* Adults are to conduct themselves in a professional and in a Christian manner. The discussions about disagreements with the district Children's Quizzing director, quizmaster, or scorekeepers are to be private. Adult Quizzing workers should not share information about the disagreement with the children. A cooperative spirit and good

sportsmanship are important. The decisions and the rulings of the district Children's Quizzing director are final. Relay these decisions in a positive tone to the children and to the adults.

## CHEATING

Any cheating is serious. Treat the cheating seriously.

The district Children's Quizzing director, in discussion with the district Children's Ministries Council, determines the policy to follow in the event that a child or an adult cheats during a competition.

Make sure that all local children's ministries directors, children's pastors, and local Children's Quizzing directors receive the policy and the procedures of the district. Before accusing an adult or a child of cheating, have some evidence or a witness that the cheating occurred.

Ensure that the quiz continues and that the person accused of cheating does not suffer

### Additional Resources
Additional resources can be downloaded at:
*www.SdmiResources.MesoamericaRegion.org*

.

embarrassment in front of other people. Here is a sample procedure.

• If you suspect that a child cheated, ask someone to serve as a judge to watch the areas, but do not point out any child whom you suspect. After a few questions, ask the opinion of the judge. If the judge did not see any cheating, continue with the quiz.

• If the judge saw a child who was cheating, ask the judge to affirm it. Do not act until everyone is sure.

• Explain the problem to the local Children's Quizzing director, and ask the director to talk with the accused person privately.

• The quizmaster, the judge, and the local Children's Quizzing director should watch for continued cheating.

• If the cheating continues, the quizmaster and the local Children's Quizzing director should talk with the accused person privately.

• If the cheating continues, the quizmaster should tell the local Children's Quizzing director that he or she will eliminate the score of the child from official competition.

• In the case that a scorekeeper cheated, the district Children's Quizzing director will ask the scorekeeper to leave, and a new scorekeeper will take his or her place.

• In the case that someone in the audience cheated, the district Children's Quizzing director will handle the situation in the most appropriate manner.

## UNRESOLVED DECISIONS

Consult with the General Children's Quizzing Office regarding unresolved decisions.

# QUESTIONS FOR BASIC COMPETITION

The questions for Basic Competition are after each Bible study.

# QUESTIONS FOR ADVANCED COMPETITION

## Genesis 1:1-31; 2:2-3, 7

1. *What was the earth like before creation? (1:2)*
   1. Formless
   2. Empty
   3. Covered in darkness
   **4. All of the answers are correct.**

2. *What happened to the waters on the third day? (1:9-11)*
   1. They dried up.
   2. They gathered in the sky.
   **3. They were gathered in one place as seas.**
   4. All of the answers are correct.

3. *What did God create on the fourth day? (1:16, 19)*
   **1. Sun, moon, and stars**
   2. Plants and trees
   3. Birds and sea life
   4. Animals and people

4. *On the sixth day, what did God create according to their kinds? (1:25)*
   1. Wild animals
   2. Livestock
   3. All the creatures that move along the ground
   **4. All of the answers are correct.**

5. *In whose image did God create man? (1:26)*
   1. Animals
   **2. God**
   3. The earth
   4. The sky

6. *When God created man and woman, what did he say to them? (1:28)*
   1. "Fill the earth and subdue it."
   2. "Rule over the fish of the sea, the birds of the air, and over every living creature that lives on the ground."
   3. "Be fruitful and increase in number."
   **4. All of the answers are correct.**

7. *What did God give to the man and woman to eat? (1:29)*
   **1. Seed-bearing plants and fruit**
   2. Birds
   3. Animals
   4. All of the answers are correct.

8. *Finish this verse, "God saw all that he had made . . ." (1:31)*
   1. ". . . and he was sad."
   2. ". . . and he needed rest."
   **3. ". . . and it was very good."**
   4. All of the answers are correct.

9. *Why did God bless the seventh day and make it holy? (2:3)*
   1. He needed a break.
   **2. He rested on this day from all the work of creating he had done.**
   3. He could not think of anything else to create.
   4. He wanted to go to church.

10. *From what did God form man? (2:7)*
    **1. The dust of the ground**
    2. The air
    3. The water
    4. The plants

# Genesis 2:15-25; 3:1-24

1. Why did God put the man in the garden? (2:15)
   **1. To work and care for the garden**
   2. To protect the woman from the animals
   3. The rest of the world was unformed
   4. All of the answers are correct.

2. From what did God form the woman? (2:21-22)
   1. The air
   2. The water
   **3. One of Adam's ribs**
   4. Nothing

3. Who asked, "Did God really say, 'You must not eat from any tree in the garden?'" (3:1)
   **1. The serpent**
   2. The woman
   3. The man
   4. The cherubim

4. What did the serpent say would happen if the woman ate from the tree in the middle of the garden? (3:2-5)
   1. Her eyes would be opened.
   2. She would be like God.
   3. She would know good and evil.
   **4. All of the answers are correct.**

5. When did the man and the woman realize that they were naked? (3:6-7)
   1. When the serpent told them
   2. When God called for them in the garden
   **3. After they ate the fruit**
   4. All of the answers are correct.

6. What happened because of Adam and Eve's disobedience? (3:14-19)
   1. God banished them from the garden.
   2. God cursed the ground.
   3. The woman would have pain in childbearing.
   **4. All of the answers are correct.**

7. Why did Adam name the woman Eve? (3:20)
   1. Because she was beautiful
   **2. Because she would become the mother of all the living**
   3. Because it was his favorite name
   4. Because they lived in the Garden of Eden

8. What happened after God made garments for Adam and Eve? (3:21-24)
   1. God clothed them.
   2. They were banished from the Garden of Eden.
   3. God placed the cherubim on the east side of the garden.
   **4. All of the answers are correct.**

9. Why did God place the cherubim and the flaming sword on the east side of the garden? (3:24)
   1. Because he was afraid
   **2. To guard the way to the tree of life**
   3. To prune the trees there
   4. All of the answers are correct.

10. Finish this verse: "So God created mankind in his own image, in the image of God he created them; . . ." (Genesis 1:27)
    **1. ". . . male and female he created them."**
    2. ". . . then he created woman."
    3. ". . . female and male were created equal."
    4. ". . . and then God rested."

# Genesis 4:1-16, 25-26

1. What is the right order of birth of the three sons of Adam and Eve? (4:1-2, 25)
   1. Abel, Seth, and Cain
   2. **Cain, Abel, and Seth**
   3. Abel, Cain, and Seth
   4. None of the above

2. What did Cain bring as an offering? (4:3)
   1. Fat portions of the firstborn of his flock
   2. His brother's offering
   3. **Some of the fruits of the soil**
   4. All of the answers are correct.

3. What did Abel bring as an offering? (4:4)
   1. **Fat portions of the firstborn of his flock**
   2. Some of the fruits of the soil
   3. His brother
   4. All of the answers are correct.

4. On whose offering did the Lord look with favor? (4:4-5)
   1. Cain's offering
   2. **Abel's offering**
   3. Both offerings
   4. Neither offering

5. What did the Lord say about the sin that crouched at Cain's door? (4:7)
   1. Sin would be no problem for Cain.
   2. Sin already mastered Cain.
   3. **Sin desired to have Cain, but he must rule over it.**
   4. All of the answers are correct.

6. What did Cain say when the Lord asked where Abel was? (4:9)
   1. "He's in the pasture with the sheep."
   2. "He's with our parents."
   3. "He's with me in the garden."
   4. **"I don't know. Am I my brother's keeper?"**

7. How did God punish Cain for killing Abel? (4:11-12)
   1. **God expelled him from his home, and crops would not grow for him.**
   2. The Lord did not protect Cain from those who wanted to hurt him.
   3. Cain would never be around other people.
   4. All of the answers are correct.

8. What did Cain say to the Lord after he received his punishment? (4:13)
   1. "Thank you for having mercy on me."
   2. "I did not mean to kill my brother."
   3. **"My punishment is more than I can bear."**
   4. "I will not accept this punishment."

9. What would happen to anyone who tried to kill Cain? (4:15)
   1. Nothing
   2. **That person would suffer vengeance seven times more.**
   3. The Lord would bless that person.
   4. That person would suffer vengeance ten times more.

10. Finish this verse: "But if you do not do what is right, sin is crouching at your door; it desires to have you, . . ." (4:7b).
    1. " . . . so let it have you."
    2. " . . . but you must trust in the Lord."
    3. **" . . . but you must rule over it."**
    4. " . . . so do as you please."

# Genesis 6:5–7:16

1. *What were the people like during Noah's life? (6:5)*
   1. They loved and worshiped God.
   2. **They were wicked, and their thoughts were evil.**
   3. They were all farmers.
   4. The Bible does not say.

2. *How does the Bible describe Noah? (6:9)*
   1. Righteous
   2. Blameless
   3. He walked with God.
   4. **All of the answers are correct.**

3. *What were the names of Noah's sons? (6:10)*
   1. Shem, Cain, Jacob
   2. **Ham, Shem, Japheth**
   3. Japheth, Joshua, Jacob
   4. All of the answers are correct.

4. *How did the Lord destroy the earth? (6:17)*
   1. A famine
   2. An earthquake
   3. **Floodwaters**
   4. Tornadoes

5. *Who entered the ark? (6:18)*
   1. Noah's sons and their wives
   2. Noah
   3. Noah's wife
   4. **All of the answers are correct.**

6. *What did Noah do after God gave him the instructions for the ark? (7:5)*
   1. Noah laughed and did nothing.
   2. **Noah did all that the Lord commanded him.**
   3. Noah instructed his sons to do the work.
   4. Noah asked for more information.

7. *How old was Noah when he entered the ark? (7:6)*
   1. **600 years old**
   2. 500 years old
   3. 400 years old
   4. 300 years old

8. *What entered the ark with Noah and his family? (7:13-15)*
   1. Every wild animal and all livestock
   2. Every bird
   3. Pairs of all creatures that have the breath of life in them
   4. **All of the answers are correct.**

9. *Who shut Noah in the ark? (7:16)*
   1. **The Lord**
   2. Noah
   3. The people of Noah's generation
   4. Noah's sons

10. *Finish this verse: "Noah was a righteous man, blameless among the people of his time, and he . . ." (Genesis 6:9b)*
    1. ". . . did everything God asked him to do."
    2. ". . . had no sin."
    3. **". . . walked faithfully with God."**
    4. ". . . built an ark."

# Genesis 7:17–8:22

1. What happened during the Flood? (7:17-23)
   1. The waters rose more than 20 feet above the mountains.
   2. All the living things outside the ark died.
   3. It rained for 40 days.
   4. **All of the answers are correct.**

2. How did the waters recede? (8:1)
   1. **God sent a wind over the earth.**
   2. The sun made all the water evaporate.
   3. The earth swallowed the water.
   4. The Bible does not say.

3. When did the ark come to rest on the mountains of Ararat? (8:4)
   1. **The seventeenth day of the seventh month**
   2. The seventh day of the seventeenth month
   3. The second day of the seventeenth month
   4. The seventh day of the second month

4. After the rain stopped, which bird did Noah send out first (8:6-7)
   1. A parrot
   2. An owl
   3. A dove
   4. **A raven**

5. How did Noah know that the water had receded from the earth? (8:11)
   1. **The dove brought back a freshly plucked olive leaf.**
   2. The dove did not return.
   3. The raven brought back a leaf.
   4. God told Noah the waters receded.

6. When did Noah first see that the surface of the ground was dry? (8:13)
   1. He opened the door of the ark
   2. **He removed the covering from the ark.**
   3. The feet of the raven were not muddy.
   4. There were no more leaks in the ark.

7. How did Noah know when to leave the ark? (8:15-16)
   1. The sunlight began to warm the ark.
   2. The birds became restless.
   3. The animals began to attack each other.
   4. **God told Noah to leave the ark.**

8. What did Noah do when he left the ark? (8:20)
   1. He found new homes for the animals.
   2. He built homes for the animals.
   3. **He built an altar and offered burnt offerings to the Lord.**
   4. All of the answers are correct.

9. What did the Lord say that he would never do again? (8:21)
   1. Let the people become evil
   2. Punish the people for their sin
   3. **Curse the ground because of man and destroy all living creatures**
   4. All of the answers are correct.

10. Finish this verse : "A s long as the earth endures, seedtime and harvest, cold and heat, summer and winter, . . ." (Genesis 8:22)
    1. ". . . I will praise the Lord."
    2. **" . . . day and night will never cease."**
    3. " . . . every season has its time."
    4. " . . . will also endure."

# Genesis 9:1-20, 28-29

1. What did God tell Noah and his sons to do when they left the ark? (9:1)
   1. Use the wood of the ark to build your houses.
   2. **Be fruitful, increase in number, and fill the earth.**
   3. Take care of the animals.
   4. Plant crops and harvest them.

2. What was different about the earth and its inhabitants after the Flood? (9:2-5)
   1. Animals were food for the people.
   2. Animals were now afraid of the people.
   3. God would demand an accounting from the people and the animals.
   4. **All of the answers are correct.**

3. With whom did God establish the covenant? (9:9-10)
   1. Noah
   2. Noah's descendants
   3. All the animals from the ark
   4. **All of the answers are correct.**

4. What was the covenant that God established? (9:11)
   1. He would never punish people again for their sin.
   2. He would never allow people again to become wicked.
   3. **He would never destroy again all life and the earth by a flood.**
   4. He would never send again a rainbow on the earth.

5. Who would benefit from the covenant? (9:12)
   1. **All of the generations to come**
   2. Only one generation
   3. Only the descendants of Ham
   4. Only the descendants of Shem

6. What was the sign of the covenant? (9:13)
   1. The Ten Commandments
   2. Noah's three sons
   3. A burnt offering
   4. **A rainbow in the clouds**

7. What were the names of the sons of Noah? (9:18)
   1. Shem, Joshua, and Moses
   2. **Shem, Ham, and Japheth**
   3. Ham, Japheth, and Samuel
   4. Abraham, Isaac, and Jacob

8. From whom did the people come after the Flood? (9:19)
   1. Adam
   2. Eve
   3. **Shem, Ham, and Japheth**
   4. Noah's daughters

9. How old was Noah when he died? (9:29)
   1. 350 years
   2. 150 years
   3. **950 years**
   4. 600 years

10. Finish this verse: "I have set my rainbow in the clouds, and it will be a sign of the covenant between . . ." (Genesis 9:13)
    1. **". . . me and the earth."**
    2. ". . . me and the animals."
    3. ". . . me and your offspring."
    4. ". . . me and Noah."

# Genesis 12:1-9; 13:5-18

1. What did the Lord ask Abram to do? (12:1)
   1. To leave his country and his people
   2. To leave his father's household
   3. To go to the land that the Lord would show him
   **4. All of the answers are correct.**

2. Whom did the Lord say that he would make into a great nation? (12:1-2)
   1. Lot
   2. Noah
   **3. Abram**
   4. Adam

3. What did the Lord tell Abram at Shechem? (12:6-7)
   1. "This is the land of Lot."
   **2. "To your offspring I will give this land."**
   3. "This is not your land. Continue your travels."
   4. "You will fight the Canaanites."

4. Why did the herdsmen of Lot and Abram quarrel? (13:6-7)
   1. They were tired of travelling together.
   2. Lot's herdsmen stole from Abram's herdsmen.
   **3. The land could not support all of them.**
   4. They argued about who was best.

5. What was Abram's solution for the quarrelling? (13:8-9)
   **1. The two men would go separate ways.**
   2. Lot would return to Haran.
   3. Only one man would have flocks and herds.
   4. All of the answers are correct.

6. To where did Lot and his family move? (13:10-13)
   1. The well-watered plain of the Jordan River
   2. Near the city of Sodom
   3. Near the wicked men
   **4. All of the answers are correct.**

7. What did God say about the land that Abram saw? (13:15)
   1. Abram could have half of the land.
   2. Lot chose the better land.
   **3. Abram and his offspring would have all of the land.**
   4. All of the answers are correct.

8. To what did God compare Abram's offspring? (13:16)
   **1. The dust of the earth**
   2. The grains of the sand
   3. The hairs on his head
   4. The seconds in a day

9. What did God tell Abram to do to the land that God would give to him? (13:17)
   1. To build a city
   2. To plant an orchard
   3. To survey it carefully
   **4. To walk through the length and breadth of it.**

10. Finish this verse: "By faith Abraham, when called to go to a place he would later receive as his inheritance..." (Hebrews 11:8)
    **1. ". . . obeyed and went, even though he did not know where he was going."**
    2. ". . . decided to go a few years later."
    3. ". . . followed his nephew, Lot."
    4. ". . . disobeyed and did not follow the Lord."

# Genesis 15:1-21

1. What was the word of the Lord that Abram heard in a vision? (15:1)
   1. "Do not be afraid."
   2. "I am your shield."
   3. "I am your very great reward."
   4. **All of the answers are correct.**

2. Why did Abram think that his heir would be Eliezer? (15:2)
   1. The Lord told Abram that Eliezer would be his heir.
   2. **Abram was childless.**
   3. Abram had a vision of Eliezer as his heir.
   4. Eliezer was Abram's son.

3. Who was Eliezer? (15:2-3)
   1. Abram's firstborn son
   2. Abram's nephew
   3. **A servant in Abram's household**
   4. A neighbor's son

4. The Lord told Abram that his offspring would be like what? (15:5)
   1. **The stars**
   2. Grains of rice
   3. The heavens
   4. Sand in an hourglass

5. How did Abram respond to the Lord's promise of offspring? (15:6)
   1. Abram doubted the Lord.
   2. Abram questioned the Lord.
   3. **Abram believed the Lord.**
   4. Abram rejoiced in the Lord.

6. What would Abram's descendants be in the strange country? (15:13)
   1. Strangers
   2. Mistreated
   3. Slaves
   4. **All of the answers are correct.**

7. During Abram's deep sleep, what did the Lord say would happen to Abram? (15:15)
   1. He would become a slave.
   2. He would never have a child.
   3. **He would die in peace at a good old age.**
   4. He would never take possession of the land.

8. What appeared when darkness had fallen? (15:17)
   1. A rain cloud
   2. **A smoking firepot with a blazing torch**
   3. An angel
   4. Pieces of the animals

9. When did God make the covenant with Abram? (15:12, 17- 18)
   1. **The day Abram fell into a deep sleep and the Lord spoke to him about his descendants**
   2. The day he arrived in Canaan
   3. When Eliezer became his servant
   4. All of the answers are correct.

10. Finish this verse: "Do not be afraid, Abram. I am your shield, . . ." (Genesis 15:1b)
    1. ". . . and your protector."
    2. ". . . who will help you."
    3. **". . . your very great reward."**
    4. ". . . and your sword."

# Genesis 21:1-6; 22:1-18

1. How did God fulfil his promise to Abraham and Sarah? (21:1-2)
   1. Sarah had a child.
   2. The child was born at the very time that the Lord promised.
   3. The child was born to Abraham in his old age.
   4. All of the answers are correct.

2. Why did Abraham circumcise Isaac when he was eight days old? (21:3-4)
   1. God commanded it as part of his covenant to Abraham.
   2. Sarah wanted this.
   3. Ishmael wanted this.
   4. It was a rule of the people of Beersheba.

3. How old was Abraham when Isaac was born? (21:5)
   1. 100 years old
   2. 90 years old
   3. 99 years old
   4. 110 years old

4. After Isaac's birth, what did Sarah say that God had brought to her? (21:6)
   1. Sadness
   2. Joy
   3. Laughter
   4. Tears

5. Why did Abraham go to the region of Moriah? (22:2)
   1. To make a treaty with the Canaanites
   2. To move his tents
   3. To sacrifice Isaac
   4. All of the answers are correct.

6. How long did Abraham wait to obey the Lord? (22:3)
   1. He left early the next morning.
   2. He waited a month.
   3. He never did what God asked him to do.
   4. He waited until the weather was better.

7. Who did Abraham say would provide the lamb for the burnt offering? (22:8)
   1. Abraham
   2. Isaac
   3. The servants
   4. God

8. What did Abraham do when he reached the place for the sacrifice? (22:9)
   1. He raised a tent, and he lived there for a week.
   2. He built an altar, and he placed Isaac on it.
   3. He asked the Lord what to do next.
   4. He sacrificed the ram that he brought.

9. Why would Abraham have as many descendants as the stars in the sky? (22:12, 16-18)
   1. He did not withhold his only son.
   2. He obeyed God.
   3. He feared God.
   4. All of the answers are correct.

10. Finish this verse, "Because you have done this and have not withheld your son, your only son,..." (Genesis 22:16b-17a).
    1. ". . . I will surely bless you."
    2. ". . . you will live long in the land I have promised you."
    3. ". . . you will be punished."
    4. ". . . I will give you another son."

# Genesis 24:1-4, 10-21, 28-33, 50-54, 61-67

1. How had the Lord blessed Abraham? (24:1)
   1. With much money
   2. **In every way**
   3. In most ways
   4. With everything he wanted

2. Why was it important where the servant found a wife for Isaac? (24:3-4)
   1. Isaac wanted to marry a Canaanite, and Abraham did not want that to happen.
   2. Isaac did not understand the language of the Canaanites.
   3. **Abraham wanted a wife for Isaac from his own country, not from the Canaanites.**
   4. It was not important. The servant could choose from any place.

3. Why did the servant pray at the well of Nahor? (24:12)
   1. The first girl that he found was not the right one.
   2. **He needed to ask the Lord to give him success to find a wife for Isaac.**
   3. He felt discouraged, and he was ready to go home.
   4. All of the answers are correct.

4. How did the servant know that his journey was successful? (24:14, 18-19)
   1. Rebekah told him that an angel sent her to the well.
   2. **Rebekah gave some water to him and to his camels, as he had prayed.**
   3. God sent him a vision of what she looked like.
   4. All of the answers are correct.

5. What happened at Rebekah and Laban's house? (24:32-33)
   1. The servants brought some water to wash
   2. The servants gave some straw and fodder to the camels.
   3. The servant told them why he was there.
   4. **All of the answers are correct.**

6. According to Laban and Bethuel, who directed the servant's meeting with Rebekah? (24:50)
   1. Isaac
   2. Abraham
   3. **The Lord**
   4. Rebekah

7. What did Abraham's servant do when he heard what Laban and Bethuel said? (24:52)
   1. **He bowed down to the ground before the Lord.**
   2. He offered a sacrifice to the Lord.
   3. He celebrated with a great feast.
   4. He boasted of his great accomplishment.

8. What happened after Rebekah saw Isaac? (24:65-67)
   1. She covered herself with her veil.
   2. The servant told Isaac about everything that happened.
   3. Isaac married Rebekah.
   4. **All of the answers are correct.**

9. When did Rebekah comfort Isaac? (24:67)
   1. **After his mother's death**
   2. When he saw Rebekah on the camel
   3. After the birth of their first son
   4. When she agreed to go with the servant

10. Finish this verse: "I will instruct you and teach you in the way you should go; I will counsel you . . ." (Psalm 32:8).
    1. ". . . and keep you."
    2. ". . . and give you wisdom."
    3. **". . . with my loving eye on you."**
    4. ". . . and provide for you."

# Genesis 25:5-11, 19-34

1. *What happened when Abraham died? (25:5-11)*
   1. Ishmael and Isaac buried him.
   2. His sons buried him with Sarah.
   3. God blessed Isaac.
   4. **All of the answers are correct.**

2. *Whom did Isaac marry? (25:20)*
   1. Hagar
   2. Sarah
   3. **Rebekah**
   4. Keturah

3. *For how many years were Isaac and Rebekah married when she had twin boys? (25:20, 26)*
   1. 10 years
   2. **20 years**
   3. 2 years
   4. 5 years

4. *What did the Lord say about the two nations in Rebekah's womb? (25:23)*
   1. The younger would serve the older.
   2. They would always be together.
   3. **The older would serve the younger.**
   4. All of the answers are correct.

5. *Why did Isaac and Rebekah name their older son Esau? (25:25)*
   1. He was a skillful hunter.
   2. **He had a red complexion and much hair on his body.**
   3. He liked the open country.
   4. He was hungry.

6. *How did Isaac and Rebekah feel about their sons? (25:28)*
   1. They loved both of their sons equally.
   2. They both preferred Jacob.
   3. Isaac preferred Jacob. Rebekah preferred Esau.
   4. **Isaac preferred Esau. Rebekah preferred Jacob.**

7. *How were Esau and Jacob different from each other? (25:27-28)*
   1. **Esau liked the open country, and Jacob liked to stay among the tents.**
   2. Esau liked cooking, and Jacob liked hunting.
   3. Esau was a quiet man, and Jacob was a skillful hunter.
   4. All of the answers are correct.

8. *Why did Esau sell his birthright to Jacob? (25:30-33)*
   1. Esau did not understand that he sold it.
   2. **He was hungry**
   3. Jacob promised to give the birthright back.
   4. The Bible doesn't say.

9. *What did Esau despise? (25:34)*
   1. His mother
   2. His father
   3. **His birthright**
   4. The stew that his brother gave him

10. *Finish this verse: "Even small children are known by their actions, so is..." (Proverbs 20:11)*
    1. "...he obeys or he disobeys his parents."
    2. **"...their conduct really pure and up right?"**
    3. "...he follows God or he does not."
    4. "...he fights with others or he does not fight with others."

# Genesis 27:1-41

1. Why did Isaac send Esau to the open country? (27:3)
   1. To tend to the goats
   2. **To hunt some wild game**
   3. To find a place to live
   4. To bless Jacob while Esau was absent

2. What instructions did Isaac give to Esau? (27:2-4)
   1. "Get your weapons."
   2. "Hunt some wild game for me."
   3. "Prepare me the kind of tasty food I like."
   4. **All of the answers are correct.**

3. What did Isaac plan to give to Esau? (27:4)
   1. A meal
   2. **His blessing**
   3. A gift of land
   4. 100 goats

4. What did Jacob say when Rebekah requested that Jacob serve the meal to Isaac? (27:12)
   1. "I will not deceive my father."
   2. **"I would appear to trick him."**
   3. "Mother, this is a deceitful plan."
   4. "Esau will be left with nothing."

5. When Jacob feared that Isaac would curse him, what did Rebekah say? (27:13)
   1. **"Let the curse fall on me."**
   2. "Your father will not curse you."
   3. "Your father will curse Esau."
   4. She said nothing.

6. How did Rebekah and Jacob deceive Isaac? (27:14-17)
   1. Rebekah made a meal for Isaac.
   2. Jacob wore goatskins and the clothes of Esau.
   3. Jacob served the meal that Rebekah made.
   4. **All of the answers are correct.**

7. What did Isaac do when he smelled Esau's clothes on Jacob? (27:27)
   1. He placed a curse on Jacob.
   2. **He blessed Jacob.**
   3. He told Esau what Jacob did.
   4. He called for Esau.

8. What did Esau do when he came back from hunting? (27:30-31)
   1. He asked Jacob to cook the food.
   2. He told Isaac that he and Jacob should share the blessing.
   3. **He prepared the food, and he brought it to his father.**
   4. All of the answers are correct.

9. What happened when Isaac and Esau realized what Jacob did? (27:33-34, 41)
   1. Isaac trembled violently.
   2. Esau burst out with a loud and bitter cry.
   3. Esau planned to kill Jacob.
   4. **All of the answers are correct.**

10. Finish this verse: "Whoever of you loves life and desires to see many good days, keep your tongue from evil..." (Psalm 34:12-13)
    1. **"...and your lips from telling lies."**
    2. "...and your mind from sin."
    3. "...and your family from harm."
    4. "...and your hands from wrong."

# Genesis 28:10-22; 29:14b-30

1. What happened to Jacob on the way to Haran? (28:10-13)
   1. He became sick.
   2. Esau chased him into the desert.
   3. The Lord appeared to him in a dream.
   4. Rebekah went with Jacob to Haran.

2. What did Jacob see in his dream? (28:12-13)
   1. A stairway resting on the earth
   2. Angels ascending and descending on the stairway
   3. The Lord standing above the stairway
   4. All of the answers are correct.

3. What did the Lord say that he would do for Jacob? (28:15)
   1. Never allow harm to come to him
   2. Watch over him wherever he went
   3. Kill all his enemies
   4. Give him two wives

4. What did Jacob say about his dream?(28:16-17)
   1. "Surely the LORD is in this place."
   2. "How awesome is this place!"
   3. "This is the gate of heaven."
   4. All of the answers are correct.

5. What did Jacob name the place where the Lord spoke to him in a dream? (28:19)
   1. Bethel
   2. Luz
   3. Haran
   4. Beersheba

6. Whom did Jacob intend to marry? (29:20)
   1. Bilhah
   2. Leah
   3. Rachel
   4. Zilpah

7. Whom did Laban give to Leah as a maidservant? (29:24)
   1. Rachel
   2. Bilhah
   3. Rebekah
   4. Zilpah

8. How did Laban deceive Jacob? (29:23, 25)
   1. He did not pay Jacob.
   2. He gave Leah to Jacob instead of Rachel.
   3. He told Esau where Jacob was.
   4. All of the answers are correct.

9. How long did Jacob work before he married Rachel? (29:20, 27)
   1. 7 years
   2. 21 years
   3. 7 months
   4. 14 years

10. Finish this verse: "I am the God of your father Abraham. Do not be afraid..." (Genesis 26:24b)
   1. "...for I am with you."
   2. "...for I am not angry with you."
   3. "...for I will never forsake you."
   4. "...for I will leave soon."

# Genesis 37:1-36

1. *Where did Jacob live? (37:1)*
   1. Shechem
   2. Haran
   3. Bethel
   **4. Canaan**

2. *Why was Joseph the favorite son of Jacob? (37:3)*
   1. He was Leah's son.
   **2. Jacob was old when Joseph was born.**
   3. He was the son that God promised to give
   4. All of the answers are correct.

3. *What did Joseph do to make his brothers jealous and hate him? (37:5-11)*
   1. He lied about his dreams.
   2. He became the wealthiest son.
   **3. He told about a dream in which their sheaves of corn bowed down to his sheaf of corn.**
   4. All of the answers are correct.

4. *Why did Jacob send Joseph to Shechem? (37:14)*
   **1. To check on his brothers and the flocks**
   2. To buy grain
   3. To find the Ishmaelites
   4. To sell some land

5. *What did Joseph's brothers plan to do to him? (37:20)*
   1. To kill him
   2. To throw him into a cistern
   3. To say a ferocious animal devoured him
   **4. All of the answers are correct.**

6. *Who suggested that the brothers sell Jacob to the Ishmaelite merchants? (37:26-27)*
   1. Reuben
   **2. Judah**
   3. Asher
   4. Zebulon

7. *What did Joseph's brothers do to him? (37:28)*
   1. They killed him.
   2. They left him in the cistern.
   **3. They sold him to the Ishmaelites for 20 shekels of silver.**
   4. They brought him home with them.

8. *What did Reuben say when he discovered that Joseph was sold to the Ishmaelites? (37:30)*
   **1. "Where can I turn now?"**
   2. "Did you kill Joseph?"
   3. "How much money did you make from the sale?"
   4. "Don't shed any blood."

9. *How did Jacob react to the news about Joseph? (37:33-35)*
   1. He believed Joseph was torn to pieces by an animal.
   2. His family could not comfort him.
   3. He said he would go to the grave mourning.
   **4. All of the answers are correct.**

10. *Finish this verse: "The LORD is close to the brokenhearted..." (Psalm 34:18)*
   1. "...and comforts those in pain."
   2. "...and blesses those who believe in him."
   **3. "...and saves those who are crushed in spirit."**
   4. "...and brings peace to those who need it."

# Genesis 40:1-23

1. In the prison, to whom were the cupbearer and the baker assigned? (40:4)
   1. The captain of the guard
   2. Pharaoh
   **3. Joseph**
   4. All of the answers are correct.

2. Why did the cupbearer and the baker have sad faces in the prison? (40:7-8)
   1. Joseph doubled the amount of their work.
   **2. They had dreams for which they did not have an interpretation.**
   3. The captain of the guard gave bad news to them.
   4. All of the answers are correct.

3. To whom did Joseph say interpretations belong? (40:8)
   1. Pharaoh
   2. Joseph
   **3. God**
   4. Magicians

4. What happened after the cupbearer saw a vine with three branches? (40:9-11)
   1. The branches died, but the grapes still grew.
   2. Grapes grew only on one branch.
   3. Each branch had grapes, but there was no cup for the grapes.
   **4. The buds blossomed into grapes, and he squeezed the grapes into Pharaoh's cup.**

5. What did Joseph ask the cupbearer to do for him? (40:14)
   1. To remember him
   2. To show him kindness
   3. To mention him to Pharaoh
   **4. All of the answers are correct.**

6. What did Joseph do to deserve his life in a dungeon? (40:15)
   1. He killed someone.
   **2. Nothing. He was innocent.**
   3. He did something very bad.
   4. He disobeyed a law.

7. What did the baker's dream mean? (40:18-19)
   **1. In three days, Pharaoh would kill the baker.**
   2. Each basket represented one year in prison.
   3. The baker would never leave the prison.
   4. In three days, Pharaoh would forgive the baker.

8. What happened on the third day? (40:20-22)
   1. Pharaoh gave a feast for his birthday.
   2. Pharaoh restored the chief cupbearer.
   3. Pharaoh killed the baker.
   **4. All of the answers are correct.**

9. What happened to Joseph? (40:23)
   1. The chief baker forgot him.
   **2. The chief cupbearer forgot him.**
   3. He died in the prison.
   4. His brothers came to rescue him.

10. Finish this verse: "For the LORD gives wisdom; from his mouth come..." (Proverbs 2:6)
    **1. "...knowledge and understanding."**
    2. "...kind words."
    3. "...words of support."
    4. "...understanding and blessing."

# Genesis 41:1-57

1. Why was Pharaoh troubled? (41:2-8)
   1. Egypt declared a war on an enemy.
   2. **Pharaoh had two dreams that his magicians could not interpret.**
   3. Pharaoh could not sleep.
   4. Pharaoh heard a bad report about an official.

2. For whom did Pharaoh send to interpret his dreams? (41:8)
   1. **The magicians and wise men**
   2. The priests
   3. The doctors
   4. The cupbearer

3. Why did Pharaoh ask for Joseph? (41:9-14)
   1. The captain of the guard told Pharaoh about Joseph.
   2. The magician asked for Joseph.
   3. **The cupbearer remembered Joseph.**
   4. God told Pharaoh about Joseph.

4. What did Pharaoh say to Joseph when Joseph came before him? (41:14-15)
   1. "Help the wise men with my dream."
   2. "You are a prisoner! You cannot help me."
   3. "If you are wrong, you will return to the prison."
   4. **"When you hear a dream, you can interpret it."**

5. What did Joseph say to Pharaoh after he heard his dreams? (41:25, 32)
   1. "God revealed to Pharaoh what he will do."
   2. "It is one and the same dream."
   3. "God will do it soon."
   4. **All of the answers are correct.**

6. What happened to Joseph? (41:41, 45, 50)
   1. Pharaoh put him in charge of Egypt.
   2. He received a wife.
   3. He had two sons.
   4. **All of the answers are correct.**

7. Who was Joseph's wife? (41:45)
   1. Rebekah
   2. Zilpah
   3. **Asenath**
   4. Bilhah

8. What happened after seven years of the abundance? (41:53-54)
   1. The famine happened only in Egypt.
   2. **The famine began as Joseph said.**
   3. The famine lasted seven months.
   4. All of the answers are correct.

9. What did Pharaoh say to those who wanted food? (41:55)
   1. "We have no more food."
   2. "I will not give you food."
   3. "Take this and eat it."
   4. **"Go to Joseph, and do what he tells you."**

10. Finish this verse: "'I cannot do it,' Joseph replied to Pharaoh, 'but God...'" (Genesis 41:16)
    1. "'...will give you more dreams.'"
    2. **"'...will give Pharaoh the answer he desires.'"**
    3. "'...will tell me what to say.'"
    4. "'...can do all things.'"

# Genesis 42:1-38

1. What happened because of the famine in Canaan? (42:3-5)
   1. People from Canaan went to Egypt to buy grain.
   2. Jacob sent 10 of his sons to Egypt.
   3. Jacob did not send Benjamin with his brothers.
   4. **All of the answers are correct.**

2. What happened when the brothers arrived in Egypt? (42:7-9)
   1. Joseph would not sell grain to them.
   2. **Joseph said that they were spies.**
   3. Joseph would not see them.
   4. There was no more grain.

3. What did Joseph do after his brothers said they were honest men? (42:11-17)
   1. He asked them trick questions to test their statements.
   2. He sent them to their home right away.
   3. **He put them in the prison for three days.**
   4. He made them prove that they were shepherds.

4. What happened to Joseph's brothers after three days in the prison? (42:24)
   1. All of the 10 brothers went back to Canaan.
   2. Reuben became a slave in Joseph's household.
   3. Jacob came to Egypt to get them out of the prison.
   4. **Nine brothers went to their home, but one brother stayed in Egypt.**

5. Which brother did Joseph have bound and taken from them before their eyes? (42:24)
   1. Rueben
   2. Benjamin
   3. **Simeon**
   4. Levi

6. What orders did Joseph give when it was time for the brothers to leave? (42:25)
   1. To fill their bags with some grain
   2. To put back the silver in the sack of each man
   3. To give to them some provisions for their journey
   4. **All of the answers are correct.**

7. When the brothers returned to the land of Canaan, what did they tell Jacob? (42:29)
   1. Nothing
   2. Simeon was dead.
   3. **Everything that happened to them**
   4. They lost their way on the journey.

8. What did Rueben try to convince Jacob to do? (42:36-37)
   1. **To allow Benjamin to come with them to Egypt**
   2. To send more money to buy some grain
   3. To come to Egypt also
   4. All of the answers are correct.

9. What did Jacob do after Reuben tried to convince him to let Benjamin go to Egypt? (42:38)
   1. He said that Benjamin was the only son of Rachel who was alive.
   2. He said that if someone harmed Benjamin, he would die in sorrow.
   3. He would not permit Benjamin to go.
   4. **All of the answers are correct.**

10. Finish this verse: "I am with you and will watch over you wherever you go, and I will bring you back to this land. I will not leave you until I have done..." (Genesis 28:15).
    1. **"...what I have promised you."**
    2. "...miraculous things."
    3. "...all that you need."
    4. "...all these things and more."

# Genesis 43:1-15, 23b-32; 44:1-18, 33-34

1. Why did the brothers return to Egypt? (43:1-2)
   1. They had a plan to rescue Simeon.
   2. **The famine was still severe, and the family ate all of the grain.**
   3. They needed to find work.
   4. All of the answers are correct.

2. Which brother promised to bring back Benjamin safely? (43:8-9)
   1. Simeon
   2. Reuben
   3. **Judah**
   4. Levi

3. What did the brothers bring as a gift for Joseph? (43:11)
   1. Pistachio nuts
   2. Myrrh
   3. Some honey
   4. **All of the answers are correct.**

4. What did Israel say about their trip? (43:14)
   1. He hoped that God Almighty would grant mercy to them.
   2. He hoped that Simeon would come back with them.
   3. He hoped that Benjamin would come back with them.
   4. **All of the answers are correct.**

5. Where did the brothers go to prepare for Joseph's arrival? (43:24)
   1. The palace of Pharaoh
   2. The prison
   3. **The house of Joseph**
   4. A storage place for the grain

6. What did Joseph want to know? (43:27)
   1. **Was their father still alive?**
   2. Did they return the silver from their grain sacks?
   3. Did his servants return Simeon safely to his brothers?
   4. All of the answers are correct.

7. What moved Joseph deeply? (43:30)
   1. The sight of Simeon out of the prison
   2. The gifts and the silver that the brothers presented to him
   3. The bowing of his brothers before him
   4. **The sight of his own brother, Benjamin**

8. What did the brothers say when Joseph's steward stopped them? (44:7)
   1. "Why did you follow us?"
   2. **"Far be it from your servants to do anything like that!"**
   3. "We did not take anything."
   4. "Where is your master?"

9. Why did the brothers throw themselves at Joseph's feet? (44:14-16)
   1. They were afraid that they would be slaves.
   2. They were innocent of the theft of Joseph's cup.
   3. They did not want Benjamin to become a slave.
   4. **All of the answers are correct.**

10. Finish this verse: "Be kind and compassionate to one another, forgiving each other..." (Ephesians 4:32)
    1. "...with patience and love."
    2. "...whenever someone asks."
    3. **"...just as in Christ God forgave you."**
    4. "...and living in Christ."

# Genesis 45:1–46:7

1. How did Joseph make himself known to his brothers? (45:1-3)
   1. He said, "You will pay for what you did to me!"
   2. He said, "I am Joseph, and you will be my slaves!"
   3. **He told everyone to leave, and he said, "I am Joseph!"**
   4. All of the answers are correct.

2. How many more years of famine would occur? (45:6, 11)
   1. **Five**
   2. Two
   3. Ten
   4. Seven

3. Who did Joseph say sent him to Egypt? (45:8)
   1. His brothers
   2. The Ishmaelites
   3. The Midianites
   4. **God**

4. About what were the brothers to tell Joseph's father? (45:13)
   1. The party that they enjoyed in Egypt
   2. The food that the brothers grew in Egypt
   3. **All of the honor accorded to Joseph in Egypt and everything that they saw**
   4. News about Joseph's new family

5. How did Joseph react to Benjamin? (45:14)
   1. He shook Benjamin's hand.
   2. **He threw his arms around Benjamin, and he wept.**
   3. He did not realize that it was Benjamin.
   4. He was happy, and he spoke to Benjamin through an interpreter.

6. How did Pharaoh react to the news that Joseph's brothers came? (45:16-20)
   1. He was pleased.
   2. He directed Joseph to bring his family to Egypt.
   3. He offered to them the best of the land of Egypt.
   4. **All of the answers are correct.**

7. How did Jacob know that his sons told the truth about Joseph? (45:27-28)
   1. Joseph came with them.
   2. He was never sure, but he trusted them.
   3. **He heard their story, and he saw the carts that Joseph sent.**
   4. He did not believe them, but he decided to see for himself.

8. What did God tell Israel at Beersheba? (46:1-4)
   1. "Do not be afraid."
   2. "I will make you into a great nation."
   3. "I will go down to Egypt with you."
   4. **All of the answers are correct.**

9. What did Jacob bring with him to Egypt? (46:7)
   1. His best servants
   2. **All of his offspring**
   3. His wife and his children
   4. Only himself

10. Finish this verse: "But God sent me ahead of you to preserve for you a remnant on earth and to save your lives by a..." (Genesis 45:7)
    1. **"...great deliverance."**
    2. "...sacrifice."
    3. "...miracle."
    4. "...helpful hand."

# Genesis 46:28-32; 50:14-26

1. *Whom did Jacob send ahead to get directions from Joseph? (46:28)*

   **1. Judah**

   2. Reuben

   3. Benjamin

   4. Dan

2. *What did Joseph do when Jacob arrived in the region of Goshen? (46:29)*

   1. He had his chariot made ready .

   2. He went to Goshen to meet his father.

   3. He threw his arms around his father, and he wept for a long time.

   **4. All of the answers are correct.**

3. *What did Joseph say to Pharaoh? (46:31-32)*

   1. "My family is not welcome here."

   2. "We worship the one true God."

   **3. "The men are shepherds; they tend livestock."**

   4. "My family will not stay long."

4. *What happened after Joseph and his brothers buried their father? (50:14-15)*

   **1. The brothers worried that Joseph would pay back his brothers for what they did to him.**

   2. Joseph forced the brothers to leave Goshen.

   3. The brothers knew that Joseph forgave them.

   4. The brothers became officials.

5. *What was Joseph's response after the brothers said they were his slaves? (50:18-21)*

   1. He agreed to make them his slaves.

   **2. He told them not to be afraid; he would care for their families.**

   3. They had to prove that they were really sorry.

   4. All of the answers are correct.

6. *What did Joseph say that God was going to do for his brothers? (50:24)*

   **1. To come to their aid and to bring them out of Egypt**

   2. To help the brothers to become leaders in Egypt

   3. To choose Manasseh to lead the family

   4. All of the above

7. *To whom did God promise the land? (50:24)*

   1. Abraham

   2. Isaac

   3. Jacob

   **4. All of the answers are correct.**

8. *What did Joseph make the sons of Israel swear to do? (50:25)*

   1. To tell Pharaoh that they would tend his livestock

   2. To promise to tell their children all that happened

   **3. To carry his bones out of Egypt**

   4. To live always in Goshen

9. *How old was Joseph when he died? (50:26)*

   **1. 110 years old**

   2. 115 years old

   3. 120 years old

   4. 125 years old

10. *Finish this verse: "God will surely come to your aid and take you..." (Genesis 50:24b)*

    1. "...to a new land he has set aside for you."

    **2. "...up out of this land to the land he promised on oath to Abraham, Isaac and Jacob."**

    3. "...to a land flowing with milk and honey."

    4. "...to your homeland.

# CHILDREN'S QUIZZING SCORE SHEET

**Instructions:** Basic Quizzing uses only questions 1-15. Advanced quizzing uses 20 questoins. Read the *Official Rules and Proceduresfor complete instructions.*

## Round 1

| Names: | 1 | 2 | 3 | 4 | 5 | 6 | 7 | 8 | 9 | 10 | 11 | 12 | 13 | 14 | 15 | 16 | 17 | 18 | 19 | 20 | Total |
|---|---|---|---|---|---|---|---|---|---|---|---|---|---|---|---|---|---|---|---|---|---|
| | | | | | | | | | | | | | | | | | | | | | |
| | | | | | | | | | | | | | | | | | | | | | |
| | | | | | | | | | | | | | | | | | | | | | |
| | | | | | | | | | | | | | | | | | | | | | |
| | | | | | | | | | | | | | | | | | | | | | |
| Team Bonus: | | | | | | | | | | | | | | | | | | | | | |

Team Total

## Round 2

| Names: | 1 | 2 | 3 | 4 | 5 | 6 | 7 | 8 | 9 | 10 | 11 | 12 | 13 | 14 | 15 | 16 | 17 | 18 | 19 | 20 | Total |
|---|---|---|---|---|---|---|---|---|---|---|---|---|---|---|---|---|---|---|---|---|---|
| | | | | | | | | | | | | | | | | | | | | | |
| | | | | | | | | | | | | | | | | | | | | | |
| | | | | | | | | | | | | | | | | | | | | | |
| | | | | | | | | | | | | | | | | | | | | | |
| | | | | | | | | | | | | | | | | | | | | | |
| Team Bonus: | | | | | | | | | | | | | | | | | | | | | |

Team Total

## Round 3

| Names: | 1 | 2 | 3 | 4 | 5 | 6 | 7 | 8 | 9 | 10 | 11 | 12 | 13 | 14 | 15 | 16 | 17 | 18 | 19 | 20 | Total |
|---|---|---|---|---|---|---|---|---|---|---|---|---|---|---|---|---|---|---|---|---|---|
| | | | | | | | | | | | | | | | | | | | | | |
| | | | | | | | | | | | | | | | | | | | | | |
| | | | | | | | | | | | | | | | | | | | | | |
| | | | | | | | | | | | | | | | | | | | | | |
| | | | | | | | | | | | | | | | | | | | | | |
| Team Bonus: | | | | | | | | | | | | | | | | | | | | | |

Team Total

# CHURCH OF THE NAZARENE

IS PROUD TO PRESENT THIS CERTIFICATE TO:

FOR HAVING FINISHED THE CHILDREN'S BIBLE STUDY

## Genesis

"DO NOT BE AFRAID...I AM YOUR SHIELD,
YOUR VERY GREAT REWARD."
GENESIS 15:1B

PASTOR                          COACH

www.ingramcontent.com/pod-product-compliance
Lightning Source LLC
Chambersburg PA
CBHW061409090426
42740CB00026B/3480